Praise for *The Habsburg Way*

"The Habsburgs, who began with King Rudolph of the Holy Roman Empire in 1273, are the most famous family of the last thousand years; and, like most English speakers, I did not know enough about them.

This delightful book explains the seven principles that underpinned their achievements. While they had their fools and rogues, apostates and busybody reformers, the majority — their champions and heroes, and the occasional saint — made enduring contributions.

The best of them were serious Catholics, lovers of tradition, who believed in marriage and children, justice and the rule of law, bravery and service. They knew it was important to die well. They gave their peoples room to move and regularly worked for peace and prosperity. Their empire grew more through marriage than military conquest. It was grand but still a bit haphazard.

This book of reflections and anecdotes takes us easily through much of the Hapsburg story. It is both encouraging and useful to all of us who love and value Western civilization."

+George Cardinal Pell

"*The Habsburg Way: Seven Rules for Turbulent Times* masterfully outlines seven principles that have influenced and guided the Habsburg family for more than eight hundred years. Through personal experience, Archduke Eduard Habsburg shows that these principles are as applicable today as they have been for centuries."

Newt Gingrich
Former Speaker of the U.S. House of Representatives

"*The Habsburg Way* might be the single most important history book to appear in our troubled times. It is a memoir that spans nearly a millennium, and no subject — from faith and family to etiquette and empire — escapes the author's incisive mind and delightful prose. The Habsburgs have accomplished many remarkable and improbable feats throughout the ages. Archduke Eduard has added another: he has redeemed the "self-help" genre, and the inherited wisdom he offers could go a long way toward redeeming our civilization."

Michael Knowles

THE HABSBURG WAY

EDUARD HABSBURG

THE HABSBURG WAY

Seven Rules for Turbulent Times

SOPHIA INSTITUTE PRESS
Manchester, New Hampshire

Sophia Institute Press
Box 5284, Manchester, NH 03108
1-800-888-9344
www.SophiaInstitute.com

Sophia Institute Press is a registered trademark of Sophia Institute.

paperback ISBN 978-1-64413-810-6

ebook ISBN 978-1-64413-811-3

Library of Congress Control Number: 2023931171

Dedication

To the most important Habsburgs in my life, my wife and children, because what would we be without Family?

To Bl. Emperor Karl, may many people get to know this humble giant of Faith.

Contents

FOREWORD

Hungary and the Habsburg Way

by Viktor Orbán,
Prime Minister of Hungary

THE HISTORY OF the Hungarian nation and of the Habsburg dynasty are linked by a thousand invisible threads. These two—often contradictory—players have shaped each other for centuries. There were indeed times when, without the other, the Hungarians and the Habsburgs would have been swallowed up by history.

Our common past goes back much further than is usually acknowledged. For almost eight hundred years, the Habsburg family has been an inescapable ingredient of European history. And centuries ago, Hungarian kings of old helped the rulers of Castle Habsburg rise to power. Or rather—to be exact—we aided each other via weapons on the field of battle and through alliance in the field of politics. Thanks to our first historical partnership, the distant ancestor of the author of this volume, Rudolf von Habsburg, saved his throne as king of the Holy Roman Empire. But we Hungarians also won the common cause: both the sovereignty of the onetime Kingdom of Hungary and its territorial integrity were regained.

A few centuries later, the Habsburgs, having become the most powerful dynasty in Europe, took the Hungarian throne. Hungary became one of a large number of countries within a greater empire, and this inevitably led to conflict. The Hungarian heart, always beating fiercely for independence, did not easily reconcile with the Habsburgs' iron will to advance the imperial interests.

We shaped each other, and sometimes it hurt.

The memories of our common history are still part of the Hungarian public discourse. The independent-minded Hungarian still regards as his forebears those very freedom fighters who stood up against the Habsburg yoke. But today "that battle, which our ancestors fought, dissolves in concord through memory's thought," as Hungarian poet Attila József puts it. We Hungarians have indeed become independent, while the Habsburgs of today no longer labor beneath the burden of governing an empire. So now there is nothing to stop us from learning from each other, acknowledging our respective traits, or recognizing the impression our own history made on the other.

Even if there were differences in methods and political positions, the perpetual goal of the Hungarians and the Habsburgs alike was always the same: how to remain ourselves through the centuries and how to make Central Europe a strong, independent player in world politics. Eduard Habsburg's book proves how much we think alike. We affirm that mankind can best find happiness in the family. We believe that Christianity will preserve our identity. And we maintain that integrating Europe—in opposition to its peoples' will—is preposterous.

So don't be surprised that a Hungarian freedom fighter (with his fair share of scars) now writes the foreword to this superb book on the Habsburgs. We are on the same side again, and we are going into battle together again, as we did eight hundred years ago.

Our common history is waiting to be continued.

THE HABSBURG WAY

INTRODUCTION

WHY SHOULD ANYBODY "do things the Habsburg Way" in the twenty-first century? Aren't the Habsburgs rulers from centuries ago, a dusty imperial family that has long since disappeared? Shouldn't we be wary of rulers, kings, emperors, and tyrants in general—and isn't this the premise on which the United States and many modern nations are built? What possible connection could there be between the royal world of the past and the society, politics, and morals of today? (And while we're at it: isn't it "Hapsburg" with a "p" instead of "Habsburg" with a "b"?)

These and many other questions will be answered in this book. I hope that, by the end, you will have gotten to know a number of very different members of my family, including: the hooked-nosed Rudolf, who in 1273 became the first Holy Roman Emperor; The Last Knight Maximilian, who lived an anachronistic life of courtly romance in the fifteenth century; the devout Archduchess Magdalena, who founded a convent in the sixteenth century; the towering Mother of her People, Empress Maria Theresia, who bore sixteen children over two decades during the eighteenth century; and the soft-spoken giant of faith, Bl. Emperor Karl, who lived during the twentieth century.

You will also learn about the many Habsburg connections to the United States. For example, did you know that the first governor of Texas, in 1691, was installed by the (Spanish) Habsburgs? Or that the territory of at least a few states of the United States was originally part of Habsburg lands? And yes, you will also learn more about the famous Habsburg jaw, our family's marriage politics—and how to get different nations to live together, in peace, under one imperial roof (just in case you ever find yourself charged with this task).

To be clear, this book is not intended to be a thorough review of our family history. I am not a professional historian, and there are already shelves of books that have been written about the eight hundred years during which the Habsburgs helped shape European history. I am simply one member of the Habsburg family reflecting on the most important principles that my family has followed—rules or principles that I believe have made it prosper over many centuries.

I shall begin with a short overview of Habsburg family history, focusing on five important dates you might want to memorize. Then I will present seven rules, principles, or maxims that I think were at the root of Habsburg thought, action, politics, and family life. For each of them, I will provide examples of how, over the centuries, Habsburg rulers, male and female, implemented these rules in their lives—and their reigns—and how even whole countries were shaped by them. They may not always be implemented in the same way across the ages. But a core Habsburg ability is being able to translate values into the appropriate form for any given time without sacrificing the principle.

Of course, not every rule was perfectly observed by every one of the thousands of Habsburgs who have lived over nearly a thousand years. In fact, on many occasions, Habsburg rulers failed to live by them. But these failures are also instructive as they prompted other family members to step forward during those circumstances—because that is also what family is about.

Finally, this book is intended to demonstrate how a set of values can be implemented into our lives and times today. I will show how the Habsburg family continues to embody the same ancient values even into the twenty-first century, long after the Austro-Hungarian monarchy ended. Finally, I'd like to ask whether our lives, politics—indeed, our world—wouldn't be better if we tried to do at least a few things "the Habsburg Way."

Growing Up a Habsburg

A LOT OF people seem to like the Habsburgs. At least, that's the impression I get when I speak and write about my family. Occasionally, when I say something perceived as too conservative — like when I praised the Hungarian freedom fighters of 1956 — I am bombarded with a storm of "inbred, marry-your cousins, Habsburg jaw" jokes. Indeed, when I wrote a sympathetic tweet the day that Queen Elizabeth died, I was called an "inbred moron." But this usually settles down, and the positive reactions to my family's history return.

I know that I move in a friendly bubble of well-meaning folk. Nevertheless, I have the feeling that they are expressing more than just "nostalgia for the good ol' days." The Habsburgs can indeed be seen as a model of a large, successful family, blessed with many marriages and lots of children. Historically, the family experienced few assassinations and made no great conquests through war, killing, or cruel intrigues. But more than this, in a time where every Christian value is being increasingly driven out of public life and politics, the Habsburgs stand for timeless things like family, faith, the peaceful cohabitation of nations and languages, and the peaceful coexistence of diverse races and cultures. For all their faults, the

Habsburg rulers appear to have cared for their subjects quite well. Personally, I am very proud to belong to this family, proud to have the blood of Rudolf, Maximilian, Maria Theresia, and Franz Joseph running in my veins.

Even if you are born a Habsburg, however, you still must become one. Today, young Habsburgs often first discover who they really are in school. The fact is, from 1273 until almost the present day, members of the Habsburg family were intimately involved in nearly every decade of European history. Not infrequently, a history teacher will lift his eyes and end a sentence saying "but this is surely something that Mr. Habsburg can tell us more about?" Alas, Mr. Habsburg, who is usually blushing in the last row, typically knows little or nothing more about it. Unlike the Bene Gesserit in Frank Herbert's science fiction *Dune* novels, we are not born with the memories of our ancestors.

On the other hand, parents do teach the occasional bits of family history; and family stories are also gleaned from elderly family members who, as in all families, pass on first- or second-hand tales about the last 120 years. It's just that our family stories are often about historic, world figures. Through my own father, I learned how his grandfather saw the Emperor Franz Joseph, because my great-grandfather, Archduke Joseph August, had married Auguste von Bayern, who was a granddaughter of the emperor. I personally had the privilege to know Otto von Habsburg over many decades (who, as a child, stood beside Franz Joseph in a famous and poignant photograph). And I have told my own children about him. I have also told them how, as a child, I met the wonderful, and deeply impressive, Empress Zita, the last empress of Austria-Hungary. She herself of course knew all about her husband the Bl. Emperor Karl, but she could also "reach back" to knowledge about Empress Elisabeth, from so much earlier.

At some point, a young Habsburg begins to read books that mention the family history, and suddenly a portrait in an uncle's apartment gets a backstory. Then—if you are a young Habsburg—you discover that there are portraits of your ancestors in nearly every famous museum of the world. If you look carefully, you might see the Order of the Golden Fleece dangling around their necks. As you get older, you may be invited to centenary memorial celebrations, in front of a statue of some emperor perhaps, where Schützen guards in traditional costumes and with historic weapons salute the family and fire salvos to celebrate the remembrance. It is hard not to be in awe of your own family's past—particularly when you also meet ardent monarchists for whom the Habsburg family is a hope for the future, not simply a reminder of the past.

In fact, I am very grateful that I have had the chance to meet occasionally with members of the still-existent European monarchies, to get to know them and to learn about how they raise their own children as "rulers-in-training." These glimpses into another reality are reminders that the current, prevailing republican form of government is not the only possibility. In fact, after a visit to these fairy-tale remnants of the world that your family knew, the normal world can seem quite mundane. After all, even most Habsburgs now live in normal apartments and houses and no longer in castles. But with such an incredible family heritage, the temptation to live at least partly in the past is very strong—which, to a certain degree, can be good, as knowing who you are and where you came from provides a solid foundation for living, even in the here and now.

So, what are the central principles and beliefs that have guided my family for eight hundred years? And how can they be applied in today's world? A few are obvious: the Catholic faith, for instance. Marriage and family. But there are a number of other elements that comprise the collection of the Habsburg values. In fact, I think that seven key rules constitute the core elements of doing things "the Habsburg Way." And anybody can benefit from them; we do not need to "bring back the Habsburgs" or "re-introduce monarchy" (though I'd never say never). I believe that living these ideas — and requiring them from our political leaders — would greatly improve our contemporary world. Now sit with me and listen to my stories, join my family for a while, and then ask yourself whether you believe it too.

The Seven Rules

1. GET MARRIED
   (and Have Lots of Children)

2. BE CATHOLIC
   (and Practice Your Faith)

3. BELIEVE IN THE EMPIRE
   (and in Subsidiarity)

4. STAND FOR LAW AND JUSTICE
   (and Your Subjects)

5. KNOW WHO YOU ARE
   (and Live Accordingly)

6. BE BRAVE IN BATTLE
   (or Have a Great General)

7. DIE WELL
   (and Have a Memorable Funeral)

A Brief History of the Habsburgs

I WOULD LIKE to begin introducing you to my family with a brief overview of our family history. Please keep firmly in mind, again, that I am not a professional historian and that my description represents my own interpretation of what is important. But if you are to understand my family even a little, you should know the names of the principal actors that you will meet in the following chapters. I will also suggest five critical dates that will help you understand our family's past.

The Habsburgs were a family of counts who lived around the Leman Lake, near the southwestern corner of Germany, in the surrounding parts of Switzerland and France. The earliest traces can be found before the year 1000; in the year 950, we have an ancestor who was called Guntram the Rich. (Wealth, of course, is relative to responsibility; most of my ancestors, despite their relative wealth, had enormous responsibilities and did not feel rich.) Guntram's son Radbot (985–1045) built himself a stout little castle in the Swiss Canton Aargau. It is from that castle that our family name is derived: "Habsburg" came either from the word *Habicht* ("falcon") or the word *habl hap* ("ford over a river"). No one quite remembers.[1]

Radbot did something else important: in 1027, he gave his wife, Ita of Lorraine, a small town and a Benedictine monastery in Muri, Switzerland, about twenty-five kilometers from Habsburg castle. She is still buried there today, as are many of the early Habsburgs. It is quite an experience to be able to visit family members' homes and graves that are one thousand years old.[2]

Radbot and his descendants not only enlarged their properties in and around Switzerland but also made an alliance with the Stauffer imperial family. As a result of this connection, Rudolf von Habsburg became the godson of the famous Emperor Frederick II.

When the pope deposed Frederick II, there was a twenty-five-year period of *Interregnum*, when the Holy Roman Empire was without an emperor. Finally, the Prince Electors decided to end the period of chaos and power struggle by choosing a harmless, somewhat aged man as their new king. They never expected that he would found a new dynasty. Were they ever wrong!

In 1273, they elected the same Rudolf — the fourth Rudolf in his family, the first as ruler of the empire — to be king. This is the first date to keep in mind. Technically, the first Habsburg "emperor" was only a king because he was not crowned in Rome. But

---

[1] A brief note for my English-speaking readers who wonder: is it Habsburg or Hapsburg? Besides the Habsburg jaw and marrying cousins, this is the question I am most frequently asked. The answer is long and complex, but briefly, while in the family and in the German-speaking world we use "Habsburg," in the English-speaking world "Hapsburg" has been used for many centuries. Interestingly, linguists have shown that the word "Hapsburg" might even be the oldest and original spelling (don't tell my family).

[2] One reason to visit Habsburg castle in Switzerland is because the cafeteria serves not only hamburgers, but also Habsburgers.

nevertheless, from this moment on, we have to distinguish between the family possessions of the Habsburgs (first in Switzerland, later in Austria, Spain, and elsewhere over the world) and their realm as rulers of a larger German-speaking territory.

Rudolf was able to re-establish the law in the Holy Roman Empire. He also re-claimed imperial land from local rulers who had unlawfully appropriated it. The chief malefactor was Ottokar of Bohemia who had appropriated large swaths of Austria. After much negotiating, in 1278, Rudolf finally beat him in the last great knightly battle of the Middle Ages, in Dürnkrut near Vienna. By the way, this was also the first time that Habsburg history intertwined with Hungarian history, since King Ladislaus IV of Hungary contributed to this victory by providing significant military assistance. In fact, Hungary has played a crucial role throughout Habsburg history, as you will see.

Rudolf gave the Austrian lands to his own sons, therefore tying the Habsburgs to Austria—which was fortunate, because barely one hundred years later, in the Battles of Morgarten and Sempach (in 1315 and 1386, respectively), the Habsburgs were thrown out of Switzerland (don't mention Morgarten and Sempach to a Habsburg ...).

Despite Rudolf's success as a sovereign, the Habsburg political position was surprisingly weak. After the death of Rudolf in 1291, the Habsburgs lost the throne; other houses governed for nearly 150 years. However, instead of disappearing into obscurity, the Habsburgs set about fortifying their position in Austria. This is the period when the Habsburg world began to center around Hofburg. Very little of the old fortress remains today, but it was around the castle that the Habsburg palace in the heart of Vienna eventually grew.

The Habsburgs experienced a number of conflicts and quarrels between different lines of the family. But they also worked on their family mystique. In the fourteenth century, they stopped using the family name "Habsburg" and began to call themselves "House of Austria"; and in 1358, another Rudolf ("The Founder") suddenly "discovered" a rather spurious document, purportedly involving the Emperor Julius Caesar, that supposedly gave them the right to rule Austria as archdukes. It was called the *Privilegium Maius* and, although everybody at once saw that it was a rather clumsy forgery, it was eventually accepted by none other than a future Habsburg emperor. To this day, every male or female Habsburg uses the title of archduke or archduchess.

In 1438, a Habsburg, Albert, was finally made King of the Holy Roman Empire once again. His successor was his cousin Frederick III, which fortified the political position of the family. Frederick was also crowned by Pope Adrian IV in Rome. He was, therefore, considered a real "emperor." Frederick ruled for a long time, and when he managed to put his own son, Maximilian, on the throne, the family's imperial position was secure. The Habsburgs would never be ousted again until the Holy Roman Empire ended in 1806.[3]

Around the year 1500—and this is the next date that you should keep in mind—the Habsburgs expanded their possessions in Austria across Europe and finally all over the world, entirely by marriage politics. Through his own marriage, and those of his children and grandchildren, Maximilian brought the dukedoms of Burgundy, the kingdoms of Hungary, Bohemia, and Spain—and through Spain, all the territories of the Americas—into the Habsburg fold.

From 1516 to 1700, two Habsburg family branches—one from Charles V, and one from his brother Ferdinand—divided

---

[3] Except for a tiny blip in the eighteenth century, but I will get to that later.

these properties among themselves. Charles V's Spanish line looked after Spain, the Netherlands, Trieste, and the Kingdom of Sicily. Especially in the Netherlands, the Habsburg occupation left many traces, which you can discover by strolling through the cities. For example, in Amsterdam the Habsburg coat of arms and crown can still be seen on churches and even on manhole covers.[4]

But more and more, the age of exploration in the Americas and elsewhere enlarged these Habsburg lands. From 1580 on, the Spanish Habsburgs also had Portugal and its overseas colonies. In the United States, the states of Texas, New Mexico, and Florida are to a certain extent "old Habsburg territories," and indeed the first governor of Texas, in 1691, was installed by the (Spanish) Habsburgs. In fact, the Spanish-line Habsburg properties comprised, for a time, not only the southern region of what became the United States, but also most of South America down to Cape Horn, innumerable islands in the Pacific and the Atlantic, parts of the coasts of Africa and India, as well as Goa and Ceylon, the Moluccas, and the Philippines (named after King Philip of Spain).

Long before Britannia ruled the waves, the sun never set on this Habsburg empire—though perhaps the most famous of the Spanish Habsburgs' global holdings, one that symbolized their spiritual faith, was the simple, but spectacular, Monastery of *El Escorial*. Located just fifty kilometers outside Madrid, it was built by Charles' son Philip II as an eternal memorial to the Spanish Habsburgs.

Meanwhile, the Austrian Habsburgs, governed by Charles' brother Ferdinand I and his successors, oversaw Austria, Hungary, Bohemia, and a few surrounding countries such as Croatia and parts

---

[4] The Habsburg imperial presence was not always welcome and sometimes led to conflict. Still, I regularly see Dutch Twitter accounts with the hashtag #Habsburgersterug asking (jokingly?) for a return of the Habsburgs!

of Italy. The Crown of Bohemia (from 1526 on) was particularly important because it finally granted them the title of Prince Elector, and made them members of the Electoral College that elected the Holy Roman Emperor—a highly exclusive club of nine (and later ten) archbishops, dukes, and kings from all over Germany. Furthermore, the Austrian Habsburg rulers from then on were almost exclusively the emperors of the Holy Roman Empire.

Running an empire was not a tranquil business. The Ottomans threatened the empire from across the sea, and through the Balkans to Hungary. Indeed, the Ottomans took a great part of Hungary after the Battle of Mohács in 1526 and came all the way up to the gates of Vienna. In addition, when the Reformation split the Holy Roman Empire along religious lines, the internal conflicts raged for centuries. In fact, in the seventeenth century, religious conflict resulted in the devastating Thirty Years' War.

But all is fair in love and war, and this was also a period of prodigious marriage-making among the Habsburg lines, the often-discussed "inbreeding" that some (mistakenly) believed produced the "Habsburg jaw." (I will explore this in much more detail in the chapter on marriage.) This is also the time when Emperor Leopold I began constructing, outside the gates of Vienna, a summer residence that became prominent in the middle of the eighteenth century and is still a popular place to visit today: Schönbrunn Palace.

In 1700 (another good date to remember), the Spanish Line came to an end when the last Spanish Habsburg died childless. After the Spanish War of Succession, Spain went to France and, because Charles VI had only daughters, it looked as if the surviving Austrian Habsburgs might also come to an end. However, an international agreement called the "Pragmatic Sanction" was made with every major state in 1713, which allowed Charles' daughter Maria Theresia to continue the family, by appending her husband's family name. The Austrian line became known as "Habsburg-Lothringen" (Habsburg-Lorraine in English), and that is the official name to this day.[5]

After Maria Theresia had sixteen children in twenty years of marriage, the House of Austria was firmly back in the European power game. But even as she and her sons, Joseph II and Leopold, reigned, the Enlightenment entered Habsburg politics and transformed the monarchy forever. It became smaller, less absolute, and less formal and ceremonial. The Habsburgs had to confront the French Revolution and then, in the person of Leopold's son, Francis II, the Napoleonic Wars. When several German States joined Napoleon, Francis perceived the danger that the emperor from Corsica could assume the crown of the Holy Roman Empire, so Francis himself dissolved his own empire on August 6, 1806 (another date to memorize) to thwart Napoleon. Henceforth, Francis would call himself Emperor Francis I of Austria, and the Habsburgs were focused on Central Europe and parts of Italy.

Francis and his brothers belonged to a glorious generation of governors, scientists, thinkers, and soldiers (In fact, Archduke Charles was the first man to beat Napoleon in the Battle of Aspern in 1809).

When the 1848 revolution swept through Europe, the simpleminded Emperor Ferdinand renounced his throne in favor of his dashing, eighteen-year-old nephew, Franz Joseph. A legendary reign began that saw the emperor training on horseback, and with a sabre, in his youth—and living to see the first airplanes, trench warfare, and the massacres of World War I in his old age. Franz Joseph was emperor for so long that the grandparents of many of his subjects had been born under his reign.

---

[5] Every now and then, somebody likes to remind me of this by calling me "Mr. Lothringen."

In the second half of the nineteenth century, Franz Joseph saw the bloody Battle of Solferino and the defeat at Königgrätz against the Prussians, The Compromise with Hungary (which created an Austro-Hungarian dual monarchy), and the development of an empire that endeavored to balance the interests of all its nations, races, and religions.

In the outbreak of World War I, Franz Joseph played a significant role. He sent a famous ultimatum to Serbia after the assassination of the heir to the Austrian throne, Franz Ferdinand, which certainly contributed to the outbreak of the war in 1914. But the responsibility for the war cannot rest merely on his shoulders, or on Austria's. Political tension had been increasing in Europe for many decades and, in the weeks that led up to the outbreak of war in summer 1914, many steps were taken by many key players that allowed the war to happen.

And then the unthinkable occurred: the legendary emperor died in the middle of the war. Consequently, in November 1916, a soft-spoken, gentle, happily married young man took over as the last Emperor of Austria. He was Charles I, also known as Bl. Emperor Karl. For less than two years he did everything in his power to bring about peace. Then, the monarchy finally ended in 1918 (which is the last date you should keep in mind).

Well, almost the last date. As often happened in Habsburg history, Hungary played a final, important role. In 1921, from his exile in Switzerland, Emperor Karl made two attempts to return to Hungary. After all, he still was the King of Hungary. Alas, the attempts failed and led to his capture and exile, together with his family, to the island of Madeira. There, the last Austrian Emperor died a heroic death, supported by his faith, in 1922.

Is that the end of the Habsburg family? Well, we shall see (at the end of the book). But first, let's quickly review those dates:

1273 (First Holy Roman King), 1500 (massive expansion), 1700 (two branches), 1806 (end of the Holy Roman Empire), and 1918 (end of monarchy). There, now you can talk competently about Habsburg history.

Almost. With these basic facts about my family history in mind, it is now time to discuss the seven rules that I believe have defined the Habsburgs' way of life. While some chapters may be longer, some more concrete, and some with more colorful stories, I believe that all seven points are equally important to understand my family. I might also add that while none of these rules or principles were lived exclusively in the Habsburg family—indeed, they are mostly virtues that every (Catholic) ruler should have—nevertheless they have been expressed by my family in a very unique and rich way.

Finally, before getting started, I want to reiterate that my seven rules are not derived from imperial decrees or any "official theory of the Habsburgs." The rules or principles are my own (albeit identified with the feedback and encouragement of many)—and this book is a love letter to my family. While you will find some criticism of my ancestors in this book, particularly where they fall short of their own principles, my goal is not to list as many negative points as positive in order to give the impression of being "balanced." There are plenty of writers, especially in Austria and Germany, who have tried to sully the Habsburg name over the last fifty years (though the "normal population" seems still to admire my family); their work can provide counterpoint for those who require it.

For my part, I will show how, despite its faults, my family has thrived for nearly a millennium, and I will explain why I love and am encouraged by my family.

Perhaps, after reading this book, you will find some encouragement too.

RULE 1

Get Married

(and Have Lots of Children)

WHEN IT COMES to the subject of marriage, I have to admit that I may not be totally impartial. For me, marriage is not simply a fundamental building block of society; it has been one of the greatest sources of joy. It goes almost without saying (except that so few people say it today) that without families—and particularly families with many children—society tends to collapse into isolation and solipsism. After all, it is around a dinner table with many siblings that children absorb the virtues that will help them construct a better, more peaceful, more caring society. Children learn to put their own interests aside and give room to others; they learn from their elders. Most of all, children who see their parents together, and witness the love and respect that they have for each other, are given strength and security and told implicitly that it is worthwhile to grow up and engage in society. You know your parents (and your siblings) will always have your back.

Perhaps these words seem a bit rose-tinted because I have experienced a beautiful, decades-long marriage, blessed with six wonderful children. I know that this is not the typical experience today. Divorce is common, and many families are very small. Indeed, many Western societies are trying to reformulate marriage as something other than a man and woman joined together (which is absurd). But then again, in public life, at least in Europe, there are few political leaders who exhibit happy marriages or show joyful families in public.

So I ask myself: Why did marriage work out so well for me and my wife? Apart from love and prayer, an important element seems to be biographical and educational. Growing up in a family where marriage and children are experienced as something positive means you grow up believing that marriage is very good (indeed, a holy estate instituted by God). The Habsburg family is very much a family that values family, so it is no surprise that I have about three hundred cousins worldwide, and many of us are married and have several children — although we also have three Catholic priests, who also exhibit love and prayer.

Today, we may not get married entirely for exactly the same reasons our ancestors did, but we are certainly in spiritual continuity with them. One of the most renowned sayings about the Habsburg family, indeed probably the most famous, is *Bella gerant alii, tu felix Austria nube* ("Others may lead wars, you, happy Austria, get married").[6] This saying, which is often attributed to the brilliant Hungarian King Matthias Corvinus in the fifteenth century, could be easily applied to our entire history. From the earliest times, marriage has constituted a core element of Habsburg thinking, living, and politics.

From the time they were called to sit on the throne of the Holy Roman Empire in the thirteenth century, the Habsburgs were

---

[6] When I was in school in Germany, I had a friend who wrote articles for a conservative magazine. He always signed them with the pseudonym "Felix A. Nube." Believe it or not, it took quite a while for me to figure out that this was a clever reference to the Habsburg maxim.

required to think about alliances and about balancing and achieving peace between different nations. My ancestors almost never had the financial resources to maintain an army large enough to keep the peace (which is why they didn't consider themselves to be rich), so they found a different means to building a power base: marriage politics. Not only was this compatible with their Catholic Faith, it was less brutal, and generally much more effective, than fighting. Marriages between leading families of different countries tended to create much closer bonds than mere political agreement. Finally, marriages with many children tended to assure political continuity, which also reduced conflict. Indeed, imperial spouses prayed to produce "an heir and a spare"—although we will see moments in the history when this almost didn't work out.

The time for marriage politics has now passed, and I don't advocate such a behavior today (though I do sometimes tease my children that we married them off at birth). But nevertheless, some of my family stories are quite instructive and can teach important lessons about marriage, happiness, and family, even in the twenty-first century.

Even before the end of the thirteenth century, the original Habsburg counts had enlarged their territory near Lake Leman to include some of the surrounding areas. This was accomplished through marriage politics. So it was natural for Rudolf von Habsburg to continue this strategy when he became King of the Holy Roman Empire: he immediately married off two daughters to the dukes of Bavaria and Saxony. But the real burst of Habsburg expansion occurred in the second half of the fifteenth century when, with three marriages, Emperor Maximilian (the "Last Knight") brought into Habsburg possession rich Burgundy, then Spain (which led to the possessions in the Americas and all over the world), and finally Hungary and Bohemia.

Maximilian, the Last Knight

Maximilian was larger than life. The son of the very cautious Emperor Frederick III, Maximilian was good looking, courageous, and daring. Even though the age of chivalry had essentially ended by his time, he enjoyed jousting, hunting, and fighting as a knight. He wrote three autobiographies, *Theuerdank*, *Freydal*, and *Weisskunig* (the first two are named after the hero-protagonists, and the third literally translates as "White King"), which gave a glorified account of his own life, enriched with elements of knightly adventure, as well as several books about hunting and other topics. He was friends with the famous German painter Albrecht Dürer, who portrayed him several times. But it was his marriage that was one of the most glamorous and romantic endeavors in European history.

Charles the Bold, who ruled the fantastically rich and elegant dukedom of Burgundy, wanted to become a king. Burgundy was comprised by what is today Luxembourg, Belgium, and Holland in the North, Lorraine, and the area of Dijon and Besançon more to the south, and a tiny region south of Calais, so it was large enough to be a kingdom. Charles haggled and negotiated with Emperor Frederick III, and in 1476 they agreed to an engagement between Charles' only daughter Mary and Frederick's son Maximilian. Their children were nineteen and eighteen years old respectively, and they had never met. But they began writing romantic letters to each other—and Maximilian wore her colors when he was jousting or fighting.

Charles the Bold never did become a king as he was killed in a battle in 1477, one year later. Suddenly, Mary was alone in Burgundy. The French King Louis XI prepared his troops to take Burgundy and marry Mary to his own son, the nine-year-old Dauphin. But, in this desperate hour of need, Mary wrote to her Austrian fiancé in far-away Wiener Neustadt: "Come with an army and save me."

Maximilian had little money and no great army. But he immediately set off with a handful of companions. As he travelled down the Danube and into Germany, his small band grew and soon princes and bishops were accompanying him. In Cologne, the force had swollen to huge numbers, but his money was almost gone. Thankfully, Marie's stepmother, Margaret of York, sent the dashing archduke one hundred thousand ducats so he could continue his march.

He arrived in Ghent on August 18, just before the French army. It was, truly, love at first sight. One observer noted that Maximilian, in his golden suit of armor, "looked like an Archangel." He and Mary were married the very next morning, on August 19, in Ten Walle Castle in Ghent.

If their courtship sounds like something out of a novel, their marriage was equally happy. An interesting detail is that at the beginning of their marriage, their only common language was Latin! When Maximilian was not off fighting the French, he and Mary would go hunting and make music together. They both loved animals like hunting falcons, and she tried to teach him (rather unsuccessfully) how to ice skate. And the princess was his best and closest advisor and an ally in the alien world of Burgundy—he even listened to her in military matters. Another very relatable element is that they read romance novels together (a bit like watching a rom-com on an iMac nowadays).

Most of all, in 1478 and 1480, they had two very important children: Philip the Handsome and Margareta. Unfortunately, Maximilian's beloved Maria died after a riding accident two years after Margareta was born; tragically, Maria was pregnant at her death. The Habsburg heir was crushed. But Burgundy remained a Habsburg possession—as did the chivalric Order of the Golden Fleece which had been created by Mary's grandfather (and about which we will learn more below).

Most modern marriages will not have the political and historic consequences that resulted from Mary and Maximilian's. But whenever men and women get married they are both enriched—and Maximilian certainly understood the power of marriage to create mutual benefits. His next masterstroke was marrying his two children, Margaret and Philip, to the Spanish heirs, Juan and his sister Juana.

It is important to appreciate the gamble that Maximilian took with the double marriage. On the one hand, if the Spanish heir Juan died or had no descendants, the Habsburgs would inherit the Spanish crown; but on the other hand, if Maximilian's son Philip died early or had no descendants, Burgundy would transfer to the Spanish crown—and the Habsburg family would end.

Philip le Bel and Juana were a very beautiful couple, but their marriage was not always easy; Juana was called *La Loca*, or "The Crazy One," as she seems to have suffered from psychological problems. Nevertheless, they had six children together, and one of them became Charles V.

The engagement and marriage of Philip's beautiful sister Margaret was more complicated and less happy. When she was three years old, her father had engaged her to the dauphin of France. In fact, when she was a little older, she was sent to the French court and was raised there for several years. She developed a real affection for the dauphin. Unfortunately, in 1491, when she was eleven, the engagement was dissolved because "marriage politics" required that Dauphin Charles marry somebody else.

When Margaret was sixteen years old, she was married *per procurationem* (at distance) to the future king of Spain, Juan. When she left on her trip to meet him, later that year in 1496, the ship got into a terrible storm in the much-feared Bay of Biscay. But the Habsburg princess had a witty sense of humor. In order to ensure a worthy funeral, in case her body was found, she tied a purse with gold coins to her wrist, together with the epitaph:

Cy-gist Margot, la gentil demoiselle,
Qu'ha deux marys et encore est pucelle.

Which translates as :

Here lies Margaret, the gentle lady,
Who had two husbands and is still a virgin.

Fortunately, she survived the storm and married Juan. But their marriage was short and sad: they had a still-born daughter together, and then Juan died, barely a year later. These were hard times in a hard age.

Philip the Handsome and his children remained as the only claimants to the Spanish throne. But Emperor Maximilian wanted to improve relations with Austria's neighboring countries, Hungary and Bohemia. To do so, he used Philip's children. In 1506 and 1507, he arranged to have his very young grandchildren engaged to the children of King Vladislaus (Ulászló) II of Hungary. Mary, who was two years old, was engaged to the (unborn!) second child of the king; and "either Charles or Ferdinand," depending who was free at the moment of adulthood, was engaged to Anna of Hungary. (Please note: there were no ultrasounds in those days. If the unborn child had not been Lajos, the boy, other plans would have had to have been made.) However, as it turned out, six years later, in 1515, the two marriages were announced—and in 1516 two deaths changed the course of history: both the old Hungarian King and the old Spanish king died. The Spanish crown was now in Habsburg hands, and the Hungarian throne was within reach.

Then, in 1526, a catastrophic event occurred that furthered the Habsburg claims. The Ottoman Empire of Suleiman the Magnificent attacked the Hungarian forces of Mary's husband, Lajos II. The Christian forces were crushed, and for nearly 150 years the Ottomans occupied large parts of Hungary, very near to Vienna. Furthermore, the young king died in the battle, leaving Mary a widow, ending the Jagellonian line, and leaving a Habsburg the heir to Hungary and Bohemia.

So as we move into the middle of the sixteenth century, there was a Habsburg, Charles V, on the Spanish throne; and a Habsburg, Charles' brother Ferdinand, in Austria. The Habsburgs' reign now included Austria, Hungary, and Bohemia as well as Spain, Burgundy, and the Netherlands.

Again, while few modern marriages will end up remaking continental maps the way the Habsburg marriages did, it is almost a truism that marriages that produce children quite literally form their families' future. The biblical injunction to "be fruitful and multiply" is not simply a divine command: it is a well-trodden path to a productive and happy life—and one that boys and girls must build together. In fact, Ferdinand I, who was blessed with many daughters, was responsible for this wonderful quote that I leave you with: "Princes should greet the birth of a daughter far more happily than the birth of sons; because the latter tears countries apart, while the former creates family ties and friendship."

Spanish and Austrian Habsburgs

What begins now are nearly 180 years (until the year 1700) of the two Habsburg lines: the Spanish and the Austrian. This is also the period of Habsburg family history most prone to comments about "inbreeding" and "marry your cousins"—and the moment when the prominent "Habsburg jaw" is most visible on paintings of Habsburg rulers and archduchesses.

The "Habsburg jaw"—a deformation of the lower mandible that makes the chin jut forward—seems to be an endless source of interest and amusement to many people, and often Americans, perhaps because it seems visually to validate the idea of monarchies as decadent and decrepit. But nevertheless, it was indeed true that for about 170 years, members of both Habsburg lines were regularly married to each other. The typical life of an Austrian or a Spanish archduchess can be appreciated very well by looking at the famous Diego Velasquez's paintings of Infanta Margherita.

Perhaps you know her: she is the focus of the famous painting "Las Meninas." But there is a whole series of less well-known portraits of her, in different-colored dresses, from early childhood to teenager years. When she was young, she was promised to the Emperor Leopold I of the Austrian Habsburgs. Her portrait was painted and sent regularly to her future husband so he could see what his future wife looked like. (The series of portraits in the Kunsthistorisches Museum in Vienna was painted for this reason.)

In addition to the paintings, the future couple wrote each other letters to get to know each other (unlike many of today's dating-apps-couples, letter-writing couples typically stayed together afterwards). The Habsburg family did not marry cousins out of some misunderstood sense of "pure blood." Rather, the goal was to keep the two halves of the Habsburg Empire together. When it made political sense, family members would certainly marry princes and princesses from other families. But still, out of seventy-three marriages between the two branches over 150 years, four were uncle to niece, eleven marriages were between first cousins, four first cousins once removed, eight were second cousin alliances and most of the other only one or two steps removed. Many of these needed dispensation from the Church.

In hindsight, and with modern scientific knowledge, we know that these marriages in their accumulation were bad for the health and the genetics of the family. From 1527 to 1661, the infant mortality within the Austrian and Spanish lines was four times higher than the normal mortality in the population, which is a particularly significant number at a time when being at a royal court ensured access to the best food, hygiene, and medical attention of the day. Furthermore, the Spanish line died out in 1700 at least partly because the last of the Spanish line, King Charles II, was severely disabled from birth, probably from a genetic abnormality. It has also been speculated that, after the end of the Spanish line, the near extinction of the Austrian line soon afterwards may also have been from genetic causes. So, from a health point of view, there is little doubt that the intensive intra-family marrying was bad for health and should not be repeated.

However, there are two small points that should be made clear. First, the famous Habsburg jaw, discussed in dental sciences to this day, was not actually produced by Habsburg intra-family marrying. If you look attentively at the portraits of Emperor Maximilian and his family, you will see that he and nearly all of them already have the heavily prolonged lower jaw—so it actually came into the family long before the Spanish line even existed, and long before Habsburgs were "marrying cousins." The jaw became prominent after the reign of Maximilian's grandchild Charles V, and, indeed, from the portraits is it clear that it was a very characteristic trait of the "Habsburgs from the Spanish times."

The jaw looks so unusual, it is not surprising that it often produced comments from ambassadors. One of them wrote home titteringly that "the young archduke complained that the raindrops fell into his mouth. His educator suggested he close his mouth, which the archduke did and found much solace." But even the Habsburgs themselves could be self-deprecating. Charles V handled his distinctive jaw with a fine sense of humor. When he had his first in-person meeting with the French king, he wrote to him beforehand: "Yes, it is true that my mouth always stands open—but don't worry, it's not in order to bite people."

Today it is thought that this genetic defect came into the Habsburg family through Maximilian's grandmother Zimburga of Masovia. While cross-marrying likely ensured the persistence of that physiological trait in the family, and perhaps contributed to the more exaggerated examples later on, it is not "the result of inbreeding"—at least not among the Habsburgs. Interestingly enough, it is thought that this genetic trait is still present, in dormant form, in our family genetics. At some future point, it may reemerge, perhaps as the result of the "wrong" marriage.

But here's a second, and most important, point about all those Austro-Spanish marriages: Of those seventy-three marriages between the two lines, it is said that nearly all of them were very happy! Of course, it goes without saying that the way the marriages were made is practically unthinkable for modern people. After all, both archduchesses and archdukes were raised to marry someone they didn't choose whom they often met only on their wedding day, and archduchesses also had to contend with a high probability of mortality as they bore many children (though this was true for all the women of the age). But within these sixteenth-century parameters, the Habsburg marriages, over 150 years, tended to lead to happiness for both spouses.

Now, why is that the case? Certainly for many of the same reasons that successful modern marriages flourish: shared faith, a mutual understanding of the sacredness and indissolubility of marriage, a common belief in the importance of family and the openness to children, similar societal background and perspective on social responsibilities—and, ideally, a similar sense of humor and interests (not surprising among people who had been raised similarly). Which is only to say, a successful marriage doesn't depend on marrying a cousin, but it does require being with someone who shares your values, ideas, faith, and outlook. I will add this additional thought: Because the Catholic faith provides such a deep spiritual foundation, it facilitates the formation of the deepest bond between spouses. Precisely because the Catholic faith is stable, it creates stability in marriages. (Which, by the way, is a strong endorsement for Catholic matchmaking sites and institutions.)

If you shake your head and smile about these ideas, ask yourself about the state of marriage in today's Western society where cohabitation is the norm, commitment is rare, partners are changed frequently, and children are scarce. Take a look at the numbers of divorces and the widespread psychological trauma they bring in their wake. Then consider again whether these older rules were so foolish, and whether couples are really so very much happier today than couples once were.

The 1700s: Maria Theresia

After the Spanish Line died out, the war of Spanish Succession followed. A threat to the Austrian line soon followed as well. When the elder son of Leopold I died, the younger son Charles VI took over. But Charles had no children for ten long years, and then only three daughters! It looked as if the Austrian line was going to die out too, which would have been the end of the Habsburg dynasty.

Charles took matters in hand. In 1713, he went to the Prince Electors and got consent for his Pragmatic Sanction, which allowed his daughter Maria Theresia to continue the dynasty by adding the name of her future husband to the Habsburg family name. When Maria Theresia finally married Francis Stephan Duke of Lorraine in 1736 (a marriage of love, by the way), the Habsburg family name officially became Habsburg-Lothringen.

As long as Maria Theresia did not have any children of her own, she was under enormous pressure. After centuries of Habsburg children, the future of the family now lay within her womb. But this was just the beginning. In 1740, her father Charles died unexpectedly. Young and inexperienced Maria Theresia was suddenly faced with an empire that had a crumbling state apparatus, a weak army, poor finances, and old ministers. There were threats all around. Archenemy Frederick of Prussia immediately began attacking the Habsburg property of Silesia, and several other powers, including France, Saxony, Bavaria and Spain, contested the Pragmatic Sanction of her father. Their goal was to carve up the Habsburg Empire once and for all. Furthermore, Charles, the Prince Elector of Bavaria, was already deep in Austrian territory (near Linz and St. Pölten) and proclaimed himself Archduke of Austria, a tremendous affront to the young empress. Worst of all, in 1742, Charles of Bavaria managed to get himself elected, unanimously, as the Holy Roman Emperor. For the first time in three hundred years, a Habsburg was not on the throne!

It seemed as if it would be the end for the heiress.

But Maria Theresia was more formidable than they had imagined. While giving birth to children almost every year—she had sixteen children over twenty years—Maria Theresia gripped the reins of power firmly in her hands. To counter the Bavarian menace, she surprised everybody by winning over the critical Hungarians. She went before the diet (a formal deliberative assembly) in Pozsony (modern Bratislava) and begged for help for her and her small children. Her successor Joseph II was three years old and stood beside her. The assembly of the Magnates swore to give *vitam et sanguinem pro maiestate vestra* ("life and blood for your Majesty"). The country mobilized, and the Bavarians retreated from Austria. She had saved her lands.

Although Maria Theresia did not personally become the empress of the Holy Roman Empire in her own right, she ensured that her husband, Francis of Lorraine, was elected unanimously. In 1745, after a brief span of three years, the Habsburg family was back on the throne. Even their former enemy, Frederick of Prussia, voted for Francis.

Besides her finesse at international relations, the young empress danced, played cards, and was very merry — a powerhouse of good cheer that buoyed the spirits of the Austrians. She styled herself as the mother of her people (indeed, she used to call herself "Chief Mother of My Country"). And with many daughters at her disposal, she formed a web of relations through Europe by marrying them off widely. Most notably, she married her daughter Maria Antonia ("Marie Antoinette") to the dauphin of France. She turned European diplomacy on its head by making an enemy a friend (for a few years at least), and winning France as an ally against her archenemy Prussia.

Sadly, some of those arranged marriages were unhappy. Her beloved daughter Maria Carolina's marriage to the King of Naples was a catastrophe and a silent martyrdom. Nevertheless, the Habsburg family was once again connected to Spain, after having lost it. Maria Theresia maintained her influence by sending copious letters to her daughters, all over Europe, many of which survive.

Despite all those marriages, and all the scores of children, the Habsburg-Lothringen family name barely managed to survive. Only two boys remained — Joseph II and Leopold. Joseph II became Maria Theresia's co-regent and was, from 1780 on, emperor.

Alas, he had only a brief moment of happiness. He married the beautiful but fragile Isabelle of Parma—and was devastated when, after barely three years, she died, from smallpox, after three miscarriages in a row. Her death gave him a grim outlook on life and marriage, and when he was married again (at his mother's insistence) to a princess of Bavaria, the marriage was loveless and childless.

When Joseph himself died childless, barely ten years later in 1790, his brother Leopold became emperor. Maria Theresia was fortunate she had had "an heir and a spare"—and Leopold himself (called "Pietro Leopoldo" by the Italians) had managed to beget sixteen children while being Grand Duke of Tuscany. (His brother, Joseph II, like his mother, had tried to micromanage his affairs in Tuscany and wrote to him after the birth of Leopold's sixteenth child: "Ten boys are really enough, your fertility should end here.") Fortunately for the family, Leopold's own eldest son and heir, Francis, had been prepared for years for his future as Leopold himself died, after reigning barely two years!

So, at the beginning of the nineteenth century, the Habsburg family seemed once again to be secure. It had produced a trained emperor with many siblings and, importantly, enough boys to keep the clan going for a long time. In fact, the branches of the family were continuing to grow because with Leopold's children (Maria Theresia's grandchildren), the four lines of Habsburgs that still exist today diverged. The descendants of Emperor Francis II comprise the Vienna line—Franz Joseph, later Bl. Karl, and down through Otto Habsburg and his siblings. Francis' brother Ferdinand (Grand Duke of Tuscany) remained in Florence, and his descendants make up the Tuscany Line—when Italy united in 1870 they fled to Austria, and many Habsburgs living in Austria today are *Toskana*. The descendants of Francis and Ferdinand's brother, Archduke Charles (who beat Napoleon at Aspern), lived for a long time in Poland and constitute the "Teschen line"—there are very few of them left. Finally, their younger brother, Archduke Joseph, who went to Hungary as a Palatine (a kind of viceroy for the emperor) in the 1790s, produced descendants who form the Hungarian line. This is my line, and you see right away that it is the youngest line. I am also a son of the youngest child of the last generation—so if I had ambitions to be pretender to the throne, I would have to dispatch dozens and dozens of Habsburgs.[7]

By the way, one of the brothers, the very popular Archduke John (living in Styria) defied family conventions and entered a so-called "morganatic marriage" (below his rank) when, in 1829, he married Anna Plochl, the daughter of the master of Post of quaint Bad Aussee. She was not a princess, nor even an aristocrat, and the battle for his brother Francis to consent to the marriage went on until 1833. But the marriage was a very happy one and their descendants, until today, carry the title Counts of Meran. We Habsburgs now joyfully consider the Merans our cousins.

As we enter the nineteenth century, there are more and more marriages of love in the Habsburg family, although a larger number still seem to have been arranged, or at least strongly encouraged. Until the end of the monarchy, it was understood that you couldn't get married without the permission of the head of the family, and that sometimes produced family dramas. Still, archdukes and archduchesses began more frequently to follow their hearts rather than statecraft when choosing their spouses.

But before I get to the greatest love story of the Habsburg history, I have to relate one of the most bitter marriage decisions made

---

[7] Isn't it interesting that we still define ourselves by four brothers who lived two hundred years ago? That's the way historic facts live on, in our heads and hearts. If you ever meet a Habsburg, remember to ask from which of the lines of the Habsburgs he descends.

by a Habsburg father—the moment that Francis II, Franz Joseph's grandfather, in order to make peace, gave away his daughter Marie-Louise in marriage to his archenemy, Napoleon Bonaparte. It is known that Marie-Louise hated the French General profoundly, as she had seen him humiliate her father by inflicting military losses. She even seems to have had a doll that she named Napoleon, which she tortured, and she privately called Napoleon "the Antichrist." But, being a good and faithful Habsburg daughter, she played her part in her father's plan.

Napoleon, who had already been married once, was surely not the husband she would have chosen—and the French never loved her as much as they had loved Josephine. But, after an initial period of tension, they did slowly grow closer. Napoleon even once said that he respected her more than his first wife, and of course she bore him his first son, the debonair Duke of Reichstadt. Napoleon never renounced his marriage to her. When word of Napoleon's death arrived to her, she famously said that while she didn't love him, she could not forget that he was the father of her first child. We can only hope that she found happiness in her two subsequent marriages (there were no divorces; she married again after her second husband died).

Nineteenth century: Franz Joseph and Elisabeth

Some of my readers will probably be convinced that the greatest and most romantic Habsburg love story was Franz Joseph and Elisabeth's in 1853. Three beautiful movies were made about them in the 1950s starring the adorable Romy Schneider and the dashing Karlheinz Böhm. Although their relationship started out as a union of love, some elements of this marriage should be considered in a realistic light. While it is clear from letters, paintings, and photographs that Elisabeth (or "Sisi") must have been strikingly beautiful, there are a number of reasons why she might not be viewed as wholly adequate for her future role.

The central point seems to me that there is little evidence that faith played a large role in Elisabeth's life. Rather, she had vague, romantic, and poetic ideas about God and the netherworld; and she adored Byron and Heine. (Her devout daughter Marie Valerie constantly expressed worries about the state of her mother's soul.) And the marriage of an emperor, under constant pressure, would have needed the support of a wife strongly rooted in her faith.

Furthermore, from the beginning, Elisabeth seemed reluctant and unprepared to perform the role of empress, which led to constant conflict with Franz Joseph's mother, Archduchess Sophie.

Finally, after she had performed her duties as wife and born four children (the eldest daughter sadly died at the age of two), Elisabeth began to travel all over the world, perhaps in an effort to run away from the court—and indeed her life.

While Franz Joseph's letters show that he harbored tender feelings toward her all his life, it is not clear whether he was entirely faithful to her throughout their marriage. Sisi herself frequently wrote disillusioned letters about marriage in general. However, to the end they never entirely gave up on the bond that united them.

Elizabeth's frequent absences not only meant that Franz Joseph must have been often lonely, but also that she was not a constant influence in the education of her children. They suffered accordingly. Especially their only son, Rudolf, who had his own sad string of love affairs; and he may have been involved in a double suicide with Mary Vetsera (I won't go down the rabbit-hole of theories about his sad end).

So, movies notwithstanding, this story-book marriage was more complicated than we imagine. Fortunately, both their daughters, Gisela and Marie Valerie, had happy marriages, which shows there is always hope.

Twentieth century: Franz Ferdinand and Sophie, Bl. Karl and Zita

Another morganatic marriage in the Habsburg family turned out to be a very happy one. Franz Joseph's nephew and heir, Archduke Franz Ferdinand, lost his heart to Countess Sophie Chotek from Bohemia. His fight to get Emperor Franz Joseph to consent to this (ultimately very happy) marriage was a hard one. But in the end, he received permission — with a few severe conditions. His wife was never to be called empress, and their future children would carry the name of dukes and princes of Hohenberg, not the Habsburg family name.

As this happened in 1899, it was clear from the beginning that the heir to the throne of the empire would not be Franz Ferdinand's future son but rather his young nephew, Karl. However, Franz Ferdinand and Sophie never resented Karl. The two couples were real friends, in no small part because they were all quite devout.

The marriage of Karl of Austria and Zita of Bourbon-Parma is the last example of a Habsburg marriage before the monarchy ended. I think that the Habsburg maxim in favor of marriage may have found its purest realization in this surprisingly humble couple. Theirs was a marriage of love that received the consent and blessing of the elderly Emperor Franz Joseph. (You can even see the happy, beaming young couple in colorized historic footage on the Internet.) Even more, the two of them really shared the same vision of family life and faith.

Karl famously said, after their wedding, "now we must help each other into heaven," which is as perfect a goal of Christian marriage as ever there was.

During the First World War, Zita performed with great warmth and sacrifice the role of "Angel of the Wounded," visiting hospitals and caring for the sick. Meanwhile, Karl was at the front. That he was a faithful husband all his life seems even more remarkable when we realize that his father, Archduke Otto (the brother of Franz Ferdinand, who was killed in Sarajevo), was a womanizer and a boasting drunkard.

When the war ended, Zita found her place at her husband's side, sometimes quite literally. When he made his second attempt to reclaim the Hungarian throne in 1921, she sat beside him on their clandestine airplane flight (the first one for both of them)—and she stayed beside her husband on the long and difficult train trip to Budapest. When his efforts failed, she accompanied him into exile and did everything she could so that the couple could be reunited with their children on Madeira. Their union was blessed with eight children before Karl's untimely death in Madeira in 1922. (Their last child was actually born after he died.) Those children appeared in public regularly with their parents, and the whole Austro-Hungarian Empire had an example of what a family should be: a man and a woman, faithful to each other, and obviously in love.

Perhaps now you understand why I so admire this last, great imperial Habsburg couple. And perhaps you understand why marriage is such an important Habsburg principle. Marriage was not merely a means of producing little Habsburg-lings. Rather, properly lived, marriage is a holy estate, instituted by God, instituted so that men and women can make happy lives together—whether they are emperors and empresses or simply husband and wife. I think marriages work best when spouses have shared ideas about faith and family (which makes, I repeat, a great case for Catholic dating sites). In fact, these things are so important, marriages that have them can work well even if they are not initially born out of romance. Romance, while wonderful, is perhaps slightly overrated in our times, at least when it comes to building long-lasting relationships. In the end, marriage is really about serving each other—and helping each other into Heaven.

RULE 2A

Be Catholic!

(and Practice Your Faith — Part 1)

THE NEXT TWO chapters are long, and I will have to ask my non-Catholic readers for forgiveness if I am occasionally not as diplomatic or ecumenical as usual. But I am writing from the heart. The fact is, the Habsburgs were—and for the most part, still are—Catholic. Period. Full stop.

It is so much a part of our identity that one could almost ask, "Are the Habsburgs Catholic?" the same way it is sometimes asked jokingly about the Pope.

In some cases, this may be rather difficult to appreciate be-cause, in prior centuries, being a Catholic ruler often meant doing things that seem manifestly un-Christian, including treating other Christian denominations harshly. But in those centuries gone by, people truly believed that only by living the Catholic Faith could you get to Heaven, so encouraging, indeed requiring, your subjects to be Catholic was not only part of your duty as an emperor, it was an act of charity because it helped others reach eternal salvation.

There is one other point that may make some modern readers uncomfortable. The idea that religion must be separated from the state has become a Western dogma to such an extent that many people, including many political leaders, now think any public display of religious faith must be strictly limited. While there may be merit to the idea of limiting state support for religion—the state can corrupt faith just as readily as faith can corrupt the state—there must also be a limit to this rule: If religion is entirely excluded from the public square, then it can have no influence on individuals, because individuals (unless they are hermits) live much of their lives in that same public square. Political leaders, in particular, live their lives in public. If I know a political leader's religious belief, I can know better what to expect, and I can hold the leader accountable. Devout Christian politicians who believe in God will be more likely to act in such a way that they will be able to give an account to God of the actions they commit during their lifetime—which, in my book, reduces the likelihood of corruption.

In any case, we shall see that most of the Habsburgs took their faith very seriously. In the last chapter, "Dying Well," we shall see how they prepared for their ultimate meeting with God.

Catholic from the beginning

There is a story told about Rudolf I, the first Habsburg ruler of the Holy Roman Empire. One day in about the 1260s (more or less when Thomas Aquinas lived), Count Rudolf of Habsburg went hunting in his forests in Switzerland. He came to a river where a priest was bringing viaticum (the Blessed Sacrament) to a dying man. The river was too swollen for the cleric to cross it. So Rudolf dismounted his horse and allowed the priest to use it to cross the river. When he reached the other side, the priest wanted to give the horse back to Rudolf. But the Count of Habsburg reportedly said these famous words: "Far be it from me that I shall ever ride on a horse that has carried my Lord and Savior. Keep the horse!"

The story spread far and wide among the simple people. There was even a kind of prophecy that God would repay such generosity.

Schiller dramatized the story in his beautiful ballad "Der Graf von Habsburg," and there are dozens of paintings of this episode in museums all over the world. Some think it is a legend, but I believe that the story really happened exactly the way it is told. (God has certainly been most gracious with our family.)

When Rudolf and his many successors were crowned, the coronation rite to become Holy Roman Emperor was deeply imbued with sacred religious symbols. Before they were crowned, they received Communion under both forms (an exception to the rule at the time) and swore on a relic of earth containing the blood of St. Stephen, the protomartyr. The vestment they received was like a bishop's vestment. More than one Habsburg ruler avowed that the moment of installation as emperor deeply impressed them for life. It was not simply a cynical political affair, but a religious event, sincerely celebrated.

Of course, the authority of the Holy Roman Emperor came, ultimately, from Christ through the Pope. So being Catholic was crucial to ruling in those days. And being a devout Catholic did not keep Rudolf from waging political wars against stubborn bishops or monasteries, if needed—and other Habsburgs, though Catholic, were not always devout. But being Catholic was the foundation of Rudolf's identity. And the Catholic faith has remained strong in our family from its earliest days.

Charles V and Martin Luther

As this book is not intended to be a comprehensive study of Habsburg piety, I am not going to examine the entire historical record of Habsburg devotion. Rather, I am going to focus on certain individuals and historical periods that best illustrate how the Habsburgs let their Catholic faith influence their lives. Perhaps one of the best places to look is the period of the Reformation in the sixteenth century.

Until the Reformation, the princes and rulers of Europe were all Catholic, so it is harder to see how Catholicism influenced them individually. However, after Martin Luther charged onto the historical stage, in a very few years the Empire was suddenly deeply divided on matters of religion. The true motivations for conflict, of course, were not always matters of faith. In fact, the temptation for dukes, princes, and kings to persecute Catholics and take away the property of the Church—which had huge possessions—were very powerful and represented a once-in-a-century opportunity to replenish empty state coffers, or to convey church properties to loyal followers.

In the midst of this turmoil, all eyes were on the emperor. Which way would he personally lean? Were his sympathies with the Pope or with the new Lutheran preachers and the Luther bible, printed in the language of the people?

The Habsburg Emperor in those dramatic years was Charles V, the deeply devout King of Spain, Archduke of Austria, and Ruler of the Netherlands and Duke of Burgundy. Like Rudolf, he had been deeply impressed by his coronation rite. In two instances, he had lain on the floor like a priest during the consecration; he had sworn his oath on Holy relics; he had received the Sword of Charlemagne; he was anointed by three bishops. And he only was twenty-one years old at the time.

Four years after the theses of Luther, the Diet of Worms convened in 1521 to give Luther a fair hearing. On April 15, Charles—after listening to the different ideas brought forward by Luther—answered in a very pragmatic way. He pointed out that it was more probable that a German monk was wrong than that for more than one thousand years Church teachers had been. He also noted that his own ancestors had been "their whole lives, faithful sons of the Roman church, defenders at all times of the

Catholic faith, its sacred ceremonies, decrees and ordinances, and its Holy Rites. They were at all times concerned for the propagation of the salvation of souls."

He therefore confirmed Luther as a heretic. In May of the same year, the emperor issued the "Edict of Worms" against Luther, his followers, and his writings. The emperor had safeguarded the Catholic Faith.

The Reformation seems to win

However, when Charles V stepped down from his throne in 1556, his "Austrian" brother, Ferdinand I, became emperor. He was a personally devout man. But the situation of the Catholic Faith in the Austrian heartlands was catastrophic. This was not entirely due to Protestantism. The Ottoman occupation of Bohemia, Hungary, and Croatia had decimated the Church and, in many places, there had been no organized Church structure for generations.

In any case, after the impact of the Reformation, in many parts of Austria, 90 percent of the priests, almost 100 percent of the aristocracy, and large parts of the population were, in reality, Protestant. Most of the parish priests lived with women they considered wives; almost every week, monasteries closed down as even the abbesses got married.[8] It didn't help that Ferdinand I had Protestant advisors, and one of the more prominent ones was a married ex-priest. (What was worse, one of the earliest teachers of Ferdinand's son and successor, Maximilian II, turned out to be a close friend of Martin Luther.) But Ferdinand hoped that some

---

[8] One very striking example is the old and venerable Benedictine Monastery of Göttweig, situated on a hill above Krems along the Danube River. While the abbey is proud of having been a monastery, without interruption, since the year 1072, in 1556 it had shrunk down to one monk who happened to be the Abbot.

sort of "middle way" between Catholic and Protestant faith would be possible. He even put pressure on the Pope to consider abolishing priestly celibacy.

When Ferdinand died and Maximilian II became emperor in 1564, Catholicism was in deep trouble. Maximilian's character was weak; he was emotional, fickle, and prone to drinking bouts. Spiritually, he devoured Luther's writings, had many protestant friends, and kept a Luther bible on his nightstand beside his bed. Although he married his Catholic cousin Archduchess Maria, he summoned Protestant preachers to Vienna and engaged them as educators for his children, especially his son and successor Rudolf II. In the battle of Lepanto 1572, Maximilian didn't want to participate alongside the Pope and Spain because he was concerned about what the protestant princes might think. After 1558, he no longer participated in the Corpus Christi Eucharistic processions in Vienna; some say that he even stopped attending Mass. Finally, when he lay dying in October 1576, he refused to have a priest give him the Sacraments of Confession and Extreme Unction because "his priest was in heaven." All of this would have horrified his devout father, Ferdinand.

The drama continued with Maximilian's son, Rudolf II. The man who was depicted in 1591 by the painter Arcimboldo as the Roman God of the seasons, Vertumnus, was many things—emperor, alchemist, researcher, astrologer, art collector. But being Catholic was low on his list. He never married but rather had a series of concubines and mistresses, who often changed monthly. His brothers were very worried about him, as their letters testify. "He strives all the time to eliminate God completely, so that he may, in the future, serve a different master," one of his brothers famously wrote. Another wrote that Rudolf collected "wizards, alchemists and cabbalists" at his court. For instance, in 1588 philosopher, hermetic occultist (and heretic) Giordano Bruno stayed at the court. He also gave safe haven to well-known astronomer and alchemist Tycho Brahe, whom his uncle Ferdinand had driven out of Styria. From a scientific perspective, perhaps this open-mindedness was justified, but his motivations may have been to affront the Faith. To be fair to Rudolf, he was a very difficult man who may have suffered from depression. He said about himself on one occasion: "I know that I am dead and damned, I am possessed by the devil." But even so, it all came to a sad end when Rudolf, too, refused to receive the sacraments when dying.

Rudolf had been deposed as emperor by Habsburg cousins in 1612, long before his death, and replaced with his brother Matthias. (Matthias' election had only been made possible with lots of concessions to the Protestants; however, he had a thoroughly devout wife, and they tried at least to begin to work for the restitution of the Catholic Faith.) However, for three-quarters of a century, and at the worst possible moment, the Habsburg emperors were "weak sauce" when it came to defending the Catholic Faith. And large swaths of Austria, with the exception of parts of Tyrol, Styria and Carinthia, were effectively Protestant.

But how did the Counter-Reformation, promulgated by the Council of Trent, take root in Austria and make the Habsburg lands Catholic again? It is a wonderful and little-known story that I think illuminates God's purposes—as well as the importance of having a large family. Although the heads of our family may have been weak, God used other members of the family—siblings and cousins—and allowed them to further His purposes.

Habsburg cousins in Styria and Tyrol

In addition to Maximilian II, Ferdinand I had fourteen other children. One of his sons, Archduke Charles, ruled in Graz, Styria;

another of them, also named Ferdinand, ruled in Innsbruck in Tyrol. Finally, one of Maximilian's own sisters, Anna, married Duke Wilhelm of Bavaria. It would be this constellation of Catholic princes that would bring about change. But the woman who really made it all possible was another sister of Maximilian, Archduchess Magdalena—the only other Venerable in the Habsburg family, apart from Bl. Emperor Karl.

Magdalena's mother, Anne of Bohemia and Hungary, entrusted Magdalena and several of her sisters to a devout governess, the Countess Thurn. Anne encouraged the countess to have little Magdalena brought to Holy Mass every day, even as a baby in her cradle. As Magdalena grew, she continued to attend daily Mass with her sisters. She exhibited great piety in her youth, and regularly prayed in front of a crucifix that can still be seen today in the *Spitalskirche* in Innsbruck.

In 1564, encouraged by Jesuit preacher St. Peter Canisius, she told her father, Emperor Ferdinand I, that she and her two sisters wanted to found a monastery in the Austrian town of Hall in Tyrol. Her father was very hesitant but finally acquiesced. In 1567, Magdalena founded the royal convent Haller Stift, where both aristocratic and bourgeois women could serve God under Jesuit direction. There, for many years, she led a life of great devotion and was engaged in producing good literature to counterbalance the influx of Protestant preachers and literature into Tyrol.

When Papal Nuncio Girolamo Porcia arrived in Innsbruck on behalf of Pope Gregory XIII to convince the Habsburgs to embark upon the important work of the Counter-Reformation, he knew he could not rely on the lukewarm Emperor Maximilian II. He therefore went directly to Magdalena in Hall. This was the greatest moment in Magdalena's spiritual life. First, she approached her brother, Archduke Ferdinand. He listened to her, and then in turn convinced their brother, Archduke Carl, to take up the cause.[9]

Then, with her sister Anna also on her side, Magdalena organized the so-called Munich Conference in October 1579, which brought together archdukes Ferdinand and Carl, Duke Wilhelm of Bavaria, and the Papal Nuncio Porcia. At the conference, they hammered out a fascinating agreement (the *Münchner Beschlüsse*), which was a step-by-step plan for how to bring the Austrian countries back to the Catholic Faith.[10] One of the steps called for Carl of Styria to take back the foolish concession he had made to the local aristocrats to give parishes to protestant preachers. Another was to encourage the bishops to put good priests into the parishes, and Carl himself vowed to replace Protestant advisors in his courts with good, faithful Catholics.

Archduchess Magdalena died in the odor of sanctity and in fact, after many interruptions, her process of beatification finally began at the beginning of the twentieth century.[11] (The story of her monastery, Hall in Tyrol, is a dramatic one and involves another Habsburg two hundred years later. We shall learn more about it below.)

Thus it was that the siblings of Maximilian II reinvigorated the Catholic Faith in Austria. But it was their nephew, a young man named Ferdinand II, who would continue their work into the seventeenth century and solidify their Counter-Reformation efforts.

---

[9] This is the same Archduke Carl who began the tradition of the Lipizzaner horses — which can still be admired in the *Spanische Reitschule* in Vienna, today.

[10] You can find the *Münchner Beschlüsse* online. It makes for fascinating reading, albeit in very old-fashioned German.

[11] If you want to know more about the details of her life, look up the article I wrote for *First Things* magazine.

Ferdinand II or a vow in Loreto

Ferdinand, son of Charles of Styria, was born in 1587 and raised by Jesuits in Ingolstadt. He was very devout and attended Mass daily. In 1595, when he was still a child, he inherited the rule of Styria from his father. When he was twenty years old, he made a pilgrimage to Rome. On the road, he stopped at the Marian shrine of Loreto, where the House of the Holy Family of Nazareth — said to have been transported to Italy miraculously — is preserved. In front of a statue of Our Lady in that chapel, Ferdinand made a solemn promise that he would do everything he could to bring Austria back to the Catholic faith. When neither his cousin, Emperor Rudolf, nor Rudolf's brother, Emperor Matthias, had children, Ferdinand II was suddenly catapulted onto the throne of the Holy Roman Empire. Now he was in a position to do more than he had ever imagined. In fact, Ferdinand II became the main champion of Counter-Reformation in Europe.

Ferdinand was helped — and strongly encouraged — in his Counter-Reformation zeal by his wife (and cousin) Maria Anna of Bavaria, who was as devout as he was and gave him seven children. A Spanish ambassador joked about her: "Sher spends her days doing penance for sins she has never committed." But together they lived the Faith intensely and showed their people what it meant to be Catholic.

This was particularly important because it was the eve of the Thirty Years' War (1618–1648), when religious conflict spread through Europe. In fact, much has been made of Ferdinand II's unyielding Catholic position during the war years. In some instances, small concessions to the Protestant powers in his empire would probably have prevented much conflict. But Ferdinand and Maria Anna remained passionately Catholic and always maintained their support for the Church, despite the problems their support created.

Henry Kissinger, in his book *Diplomacy*, contrasts Ferdinand II with his nemesis in France, the legendary and politically agile Secretary of State for Foreign affairs, Cardinal Richelieu. The latter, although he was a Catholic cardinal, believed that everything should be subordinated to the interests of the state, including the interests of the Catholic Church. He did not understand Ferdinand at all; he was mystified as to why Ferdinand was unwilling to make agreements with concessions about faith. But there is a very telling quote from Ferdinand that shows his motivation: "Non-Catholics think me unfeeling for banning heresy. But I love them rather than I hate them. If I didn't love them, I would freely leave them in their error."

To a large extent, Austria—and the Habsburg family itself—is still largely Catholic because Ferdinand II did not yield to the politics of his age, but rather lived his own faith fervently. Indeed, as an expression of his own devotion, Ferdinand II did something remarkable for Vienna. Ferdinand sent architects to Loreto in Italy to measure out the exact proportions and take note of the materials of the House of Nazareth there. He then had an exact copy constructed in the center of the *Augustinerkirche* ("Augustiner Church"), directly beside the Hofburg. In 1627, his wife dedicated this Loreto Chapel, and over the next 150 years, it became one of the most popular Marian pilgrimage places in Austria—and indeed, "Loreto chapels" were eventually constructed all over the Habsburg lands. It also played a central religious role in the Habsburg family itself. Empresses until Maria Theresia prayed there before childbirth, and the *Augustinerkirche* became the marriage location par excellence for the Habsburgs (Empress Elisabeth was married there). It also received the hearts of the Habsburgs, after their death, to symbolize that the hearts of the Habsburgs were "always with Mary." Alas, if you visit the *Augustinerkirche* today and look for the Loreto chapel you will not find it—another sad story, which we will learn more about shortly.

RULE 2B

Be Catholic!

(and Practice Your Faith — Part 2)

Leopold I

THE PINNACLE OF the Catholic Faith in Habsburg lands can be found under Emperor Leopold I. Leopold had wanted to become a priest as a young man. But he was destined, through the surprising (childless) death of his emperor-brother, to rule for the entire second half of the seventeenth century. In fact, because he died in 1705, he actually brought the Habsburgs into the eighteenth century.

His was the glory of Baroque piety in the last shining epoch before Enlightenment. Under Leopold, the Turks were beaten at Vienna in 1683 and subsequently pushed back out of Hungary and parts of the Balkans, which initiated the slow decline of the Ottoman Empire. During his reign, splendid churches were built to adorn Vienna—as well as a Baroque pious pillar, the *Pestsäule* on Graben Street, as a thank-offering to God for the deliverance from the plague. (Many other places in his lands would erect similar pillars.)

In addition, the liturgy of the church shaped everyday life as it never did again in Habsburg lands. The emperor began his day by hearing three Masses, reading along in his missal.

He presided over countless Masses, processions, and feast days in the capital. He and his family were visibly Catholic, as was his entire court. And the emperor brought the entire country with him. (It is fun to read the comments of the French Ambassador to Vienna. He once complained that he had spent "one hundred hours on his knees after Palm Sunday" until the end of the Easter celebrations. A modern diplomat to the Holy See might perhaps sympathize, though he'd spend far less time kneeling.)

This was also a time of renewed Eucharistic devotion in Austria, so much so that a new acrostic became popular: *EUCHARIS-TIA*—an anagram for *HIC EST AUSTRIA*: Austria is Eucharist. All this occurred just a few years after Maximilian had given up attending Eucharistic procession. Never mind the emperor: God's power is indeed great.

If you ever find yourself in Vienna, there are dozens of places—in churches, in buildings, on facades—where you can still see the "*L I*" logo of the emperor. But to really appreciate the overwhelming presence of the imperial couple, visit the *Rochuskirche* ("St. Roch church") on *Landstrasse* in Vienna. There you will find not only the initials of the emperor, high up on the ceiling, but also, in a side chapel on the left, a painting which depicts the emperor and his family, with their many children, kneeling in front of Vienna. Leopold is easily recognizable by his large wig, even larger chin (he was the last Habsburg to have the visible Habsburg Jaw), and his huge, drooping Charles Bronson moustache. Around the altar, you will be able to see two windows with the names of emperor and empress written beneath them through which the Habsburg family could observe the Holy Mass, discreetly, whenever they wanted. (Fittingly, the church now also contains a painting and a relic of Leopold's very devout descendant, Bl. Emperor Karl.)

Since the Enlightenment, many make fun of Baroque piety. But if getting to Heaven is really the aim of a Christian life, leaders who live their faith visibly are very important. Mankind is damaged by Original Sin, and processions, rosaries, novenas, devotion to the Sacred Heart, and other forms of so-called "popular piety" are all incredibly useful tools to combat sin as we walk along the path to Heaven. It is also very encouraging to see them publicly embraced.

Maria Theresia

If the reign of Leopold I was the pinnacle of Catholic faith in Habsburg lands, many other Habsburgs were devout but faced obstacles to championing their Faith. For example, Maria Theresia made pilgrimages, prayed at the Loreto shrine in Vienna before each of her sixteen births, and ordered prayer vigils and adorations all over the country when she was going into labor. Most importantly, it was under her reign that the Catholic Church in Hungary was quite literally rebuilt: Many churches and monasteries were constructed, and, indeed, many of the liturgical vestments in these churches were made from ball gowns that she herself donated, many of which are preserved to this day.

But her faith was also very strict. She closely managed her children's devotions and even sent them letters from afar long after they were married. In fact, some of them later admitted they were terrified of their mother's regular admonitions.

Meanwhile, her husband, Francis of Lorraine, was not only devoted to the Enlightenment, but actually a Freemason — despite the fact that Pope Clemens XII had condemned masonry clearly in 1738 in his damning bull, *In Eminenti Apostolatus Specula*.[12] The sons and daughters of Maria Theresia and Francis were raised between the very severe faith of their mother and the very humanistic faith of their father. It is perhaps no wonder that many of them preferred their father's faith.

Joseph II

One of their children who was consumed with Enlightenment ideas was Joseph II. From the beginning, Joseph was a hard-working, austere, mechanically minded man who believed in a clockwork vision of the Habsburg Empire. He is known to have read, secretly and behind his mother's back, Voltaire and other writers critical of the Catholic Church. He was greatly influenced by the writer Muratori, who vehemently criticized Baroque piety and encouraged anti-clerical and Jansenist thinking. (Joseph joked about the fact that the education of a future emperor seemed to consist entirely of "being an altar boy and going to confession regularly.")

Jansenism had developed in France in the seventeenth century as a reaction to the Protestant idea that mankind is too horrible and depraved to contribute even the slightest bit to its salvation, but must only be saved by grace. The central theories of Jansenism were condemned by Pope Innocent X. Nevertheless, it led to a great interiorizing of devotion and prayer and opposition to exterior works of popular piety like processions, devotions, and adoration. By the

---

[12] Francis had been admitted to the Freemason Lodge in The Hague in 1731 by the British ambassador. He became a Masonic apprentice and later a Master Mason. In 1742, the first Vienna Lodge, the Three Canons, was founded by a close friend of Frederick of Prussia, who was also a Mason. It is said that Francis Stephan was also a member of that lodge, and that when it was raided by troops in 1743, he barely escaped through the back door.

time Joseph II came under its influence, Jansenists had developed a strong dislike for the Jesuits who, at that time, still encouraged popular devotion like the Sacred Heart prayers.

Joseph was also an ardent admirer of Frederick II of Prussia for his reforms (though Frederick always called Joseph "the Empire's altar boy" behind his back). If only Joseph had behaved like an altar boy. In fact, he conducted a series of affairs and frequented prostitutes. Worse, when Joseph became emperor in 1780, his worldliness and skepticism led him to attack the Church. The Carthusian Monastery of Mauerbach attracted Joseph's particular ire. He railed against Mauerbach and other "useless" monasteries that did nothing but pray (and didn't advance state-building), and, on January 12, 1782, he issued his Decree on the Dissolution of Religious Orders. All monasteries that didn't perform useful, worldly functions (schooling children, caring for the sick, etc.) were to be closed down and their properties moved into a fund. Consider the religious landscape of Joseph's era. In 1770, there were 2,163 monasteries and about forty-five thousand monks and nuns spread across the Habsburg lands.

Nowadays, it is hard to imagine a world so rich in spiritual culture. (In Austria today there are only 192 religious communities and about five thousand vowed religious.) Among these two thousand monasteries were hundreds of contemplative religious houses: Capuchins, Carthusians, Camaldolese, Brothers of the Forest, Hermits, Carmelites, Poor Clares, Capuchin Sisters, Paulists, Premonstratensians, and scores of others. But judgment had been served on places of "uselessness." One hundred forty contemplative houses were closed in one year; one thousand five hundred religious sisters and brothers were displaced and, in many cases, simply had to go home, if they were unable to find a place at another more "useful" monastery.

In 1782, Pope Pius VI made a fruitless journey to Vienna to discuss the matter with the emperor. When the Pope departed, Joseph courteously accompanied him to the monastery of Maria Brunn, gave him a goodbye present—and then immediately shut down that very monastery the moment the Pope was out of sight.

Dissolutions continued and even increased. In 1783 a second wave began that engulfed another eight hundred houses in Austria and in the crown's other lands—for example, the mighty Abbey of Pannonhalma in Hungary was closed in 1786; and in today's Poland only the Sanctuary of Jasna Gora survived the purges. In 1791, Emperor Joseph II conceived a third wave of 450 closures; only his timely death prevented them from being carried out. In the end, nearly half of all religious houses were closed, and not a single contemplative religious order was left in the Austrian lands.

Reading the heart-wrenching descriptions of these closings is deeply distressing. The monks and nuns were devastated; it seemed as if all their praying and begging had amounted to nothing.[13] Even today, throughout the former empire the legacy of Joseph's "massacre of monasteries" is evident. For instance, the palace on Budapest Castle hill where the Hungarian Prime Minister works is the old *Karmelita Kolostor*, a contemplative monastery closed by Joseph II. One of the saddest closures, for family reasons, was the Monastery in Hall in Tyrol founded by the Venerable Archduchess Magdalena two hundred years before. After it was shut down, it became, among other things, a Sparkasse bank. And the magnificent Loreto chapel in the *Augustinerkirche*, erected under Ferdinand II 150 years prior, was closed and razed to the ground in

---

[13] My article about Joseph II, "They did nothing but pray," in *First Things* magazine provides more detail.

1784. Joseph transferred the heart relics of the Habsburgs into a side chapel, a former chapter hall.

Although Joseph II certainly bears responsibility for these closings, it is often forgotten that Maria Theresia herself had started closing down monasteries in the 1760s, in Austrian Lombardy. She also had begun the abolishing of religious holidays and processions. Pious as she was, she was not immune to Jansenism. In some ways, Joseph only continued, and further radicalized, his mother's own ideas.

The policies that Joseph II implemented to undermine Catholic Faith and popular piety were especially grievous because he was named after the devout and humble St. Joseph, for whom his mother had a great devotion; she had prayed a lot to him before Joseph's birth. But this same man eliminated twenty-four saints' feasts (mostly in order to lift the productivity of the farmers), reduced hours of adoration, and practically abolished processions. He also introduced, for the first time, civil marriage.

I do want to be careful about passing judgment on Joseph II's personal faith. He may have been devout in his own fashion: he went to Mass and to Confession—and at least he never seems to have been a Freemason, despite having been surrounded by Masonic advisors and having implemented many Masonic ideas. In fact, he referred to Freemasonry as "a charlatanry." Furthermore, thanks to Joseph, Austria has a system of parishes covering the entire country so that "no citizen should have to walk more than an hour in order to go to Sunday Mass," as he put it himself. Institutions like the priest's seminary in Pest still exist today and witness to the positive aspects of his religious legacy, but this system was developed less out of piety than because Joseph expected his priests to preach on useful matters and teach his subjects to be good and useful citizens. On the other hand, his Patent of Toleration from 1781 allowed faithful of other religious communities to practice their beliefs freely.

But whatever his personal beliefs, the destructive consequences of Joseph's legacy with respect to the broader Church, faith, and religious communities is an undisputed part of the historical record.

Leopold II

In his short reign of two years as emperor, Joseph's brother Leopold II was able to repair some of the damage that Joseph had done. He even reopened a few monasteries, which is particularly noteworthy because when he was still only the Grand Duke of Tuscany, he himself had closed down 130 of the 345 monasteries in his Grand Duchy (two thousand of 6,800 monks were sent home) and half of the convents, led a campaign against popular piety, and was especially vicious in his attacks on the devotion to the Sacred Heart. In fact, as Grand Duke of Tuscany he even hosted the infamous Synod of Pistoia in 1786, which reached a series of conclusions about papal authority, infallibility, and other ecclesiastical matters that were later condemned by the Church. (Leopold, despite having had sixteen children, also had at least one long-time mistress for whom he even prepared a palace not too far away from his, with his portrait in her bedchamber.)

The nineteenth century

With this as background, it is little wonder that the next Habsburg generation, comprised of Leopold's sixteen children, carried the seeds of Enlightenment and Jansenism wherever they went. This produced many challenges for the Faith. However, as we have seen, it also must be said that some of the modernizations and reforms that were instituted produced a positive impact on the empire. Francis II and his brothers were raised studying the sciences and literature and reading French philosophers. Indeed, many of them became great reformers in their fields. The Archduke Charles excelled in military matters; Archduke Joseph improved the infrastructure and turned Budapest into an economic powerhouse in Hungary; and Archduke John in Styria and Archduke Rainer as Viceroy of the Kingdom of Lombardy-Venetia were more interested in the concrete life circumstances than perhaps their forebears were. They each helped modernize their countries as they thought best, bringing them firmly into the nineteenth century.

However, there does seem to have been a noticeable lull in visible devotion and piety in much of the Habsburg family, and for quite some time. They may have been Catholic, but it was a liberal Catholicism suspicious of piety in general, and the Jesuits in particular. For example, Archduke John, son of Leopold II and brother to Emperor Francis — while personally a devout man who believed in God, prayed, and was touched by liturgy and popular piety — said the "extreme" spirituality of the Jesuits was good for "simple, overseas subjects, but not for thinking people in Europe." He also preferred to refer to God as "the Godhead" or "the Supreme Being," in sympathy with the spirit of the age. Francis II, another of the brothers, famously quipped about the Russian Czar's proposed Holy Alliance between the Christian rulers of Europe that he wasn't sure whether he should discuss the idea with his cabinet or his confessor. (This same Francis openly had a mistress that even his faithful wife mentions in her letters to him: "You rascal, have you been with the Spintin again?"[14])

---

[14] It must be said that his third wife had such a tender constitution that he couldn't have real marital relations with her. But still ...

This was also the last period of priestly vocations in our family for a very long time. Leopold's son Rudolf (1788–1831) was the Bishop of Olmütz and subsequently a cardinal; and Karl Ambrosius of Austria-Este was the Archbishop of Esztergom and the Primate of Hungary; he contracted typhoid when he personally cared for the wounded soldiers after the Battle of Győr (Raab) against Napoleon and died in 1809. Today we would say he made an "offer of life."

But after that there were no further priestly vocations in this most Catholic of families, despite the dozens and dozens of young men who were born. In fact, the first Habsburg to enter the priesthood after nearly two hundred years was my own brother, Fr. Paul Habsburg, who was ordained a priest in December 2001. (Since then, we've had three priests and a fourth one is being trained. God has once again been generous with our family.)

Despite the ebbing of Habsburg public piety, some imperial expressions of faith did certainly remain. Franz Joseph, who ruled from 1848–1916, was most definitely Catholic and visibly devout, and he could be seen practicing his faith in public at feasts and processions. In fact, the emperor himself washed the feet of twelve poor on Holy Thursday, and at least once, Franz Joseph left a deep mark on Church history. In the papal conclave of 1903, the emperor used his so-called *jus exclusivae* to veto a candidate to the papacy. When, after several ballots on August 2, the Cardinal Secretary of State was leading in the votes, the Cardinal of Cracow spoke on behalf of the emperor and declared a veto against the then-favorite, Cardinal Rampolla. The next day, support for Rampolla fell back and Cardinal-Patriarch Giuseppe Sarto, the future Saint Pius X, was elected as the new pontiff two days later. So the action by the old Habsburg emperor led ultimately to a pope who became a saint. But it was the last time the Habsburgs used their right to veto a papal election.

Why did Franz Joseph use his *Ius Exclusivae*? Some speculate that Rampolla was "a liberal" or even "a Freemason." Today historians say simply because he was "close to the French" and because of his policy in support of the aspirations of the Slavs who were causing unrest in the Balkans. But in any case, the intervention caused anger and uproar among the cardinals, and six months after his election Pope Pius X himself abolished the veto right for the Habsburgs, or any other worldly power.

Franz Joseph's brother, Charles Ludwig, was also very pious. In fact, he went on a pilgrimage to the Holy Land where unfortunately he died after drinking contaminated water from the Jordan River. But his faith lived on, in the two shining examples of his son, Franz Ferdinand, and his grandson, Bl. Karl.

Franz Ferdinand was the heir to the throne who was assassinated in Sarajevo in 1914. He and his wife Sophie Chotek were both deeply devout. In fact, when they were assassinated, both were in the fourth of their Nine First Fridays Devotion of Reparation to The Sacred Heart of Our Lord, and each was carrying a medal of the Sacred Heart—which represented the same Sacred Heart devotion that Leopold II had fought against in Tuscany.

Karl, who would later become the last emperor of Austria-Hungary, and his wife Zita were also devoted to the Sacred Heart. The two couples met regularly and together devised a plan to heal an old wound in the Habsburg family history. They petitioned Emperor Franz Joseph to restore Archduchess Magdalena's monastery in Hall in Tyrol that had been closed by Joseph II. He agreed. Unfortunately, Franz Ferdinand died before the plan was implemented. But his nephew made it a reality. In 1915, Bl. Emperor Karl rededicated the monastery and invited a new order of nuns from Belgium—the Daughters of the Sacred Heart of Jesus—to reside in the same sacred space where his saintly ancestor had lived

350 years before. Adoration of the Most Blessed Sacrament continues at this convent even today.

There is an interesting and strange story that ties St. Pius X to Karl and Zita and Franz Ferdinand. In 1911, just before her marriage, Zita had an audience with the Pope. He congratulated her on marrying the heir to the throne. She corrected him, saying, "No, your holiness, the heir to the throne is Franz Ferdinand." The Pope replied, "No, Karl will be the successor of Franz Joseph" and added: "He is God's reward for everything that Austria has done for the church." When Franz Ferdinand was assassinated in Sarajevo, Zita understood the prophecy of the Pope. And Karl became the reward—as the only Habsburg beatified until today.

The deep devotion and sanctity of Bl. Karl and Zita are well known, and I don't have much to add. Suffice it to say that one has been declared a Blessed of the Church and will surely be made a saint, and the process for the other has now begun. Faith and piety, both in public and in private, were a central part of their marriage and their love story. Even in the trenches and the transport trains of World War I, Karl would always have an image of the Sacred Heart and a bottle of holy water resting on his nightstand. He and Zita both kept their rosaries always close at hand; they prayed together and went to Holy Mass almost daily. In fact, the few days where Holy Mass was denied to them—as on the ship that brought them into exile on Madeira—were a hard trial.

When Bl. Karl was beatified by Pope John Paul II in St. Peter's Square, hundreds of family members were present. Poignantly, the Pope did not choose the day of his death, April 1, as his feast day but rather October 21, the day of his marriage. We can assume he hoped both Karl and Zita would someday be canonized as a saintly couple—and indeed, the cause of Zita's beatification has now begun, so there is hope to have this couple at the "honor of the altars" in the not-too-distant future.

After eight hundred years of the intimate Habsburg presence in European politics, members of our family are still putting their faith first and making it the center of their lives. Even if many Habsburg rulers were imperfect Catholics, Christ came to save sinners. And that is a very hopeful thought.

RULE 3

BELIEVE IN
THE EMPIRE

(and in Subsidiarity)

EMPIRES HAVE GOTTEN something of a bad rap lately. I blame George Lucas. In *Star Wars*, a huge galaxy is tyrannized by a scheming, cackling emperor who outmaneuvers a weak democracy (where every planet is aesthetically different, but morally the same) and brutally controls it with evil stormtroopers. Thank God for the Rebellion that challenges the tyrant and finally beats him.

The Holy Roman Empire—and thus the reality that shaped, and was shaped by, the Habsburgs for hundreds of years—was a wholly different beast. For science fiction fans, the empire in Frank Herbert's *Dune* novels is much closer to it: Herbert's emperor does not have absolute power; he can only keep the galaxy together with diplomacy between the ruling Houses (and a lot of evil backstabbing—well, nobody's perfect; see the chapters above).

Before we turn to the history, I want to discuss a very important word: subsidiarity. It is the key word and principle for understanding the Holy Roman Empire and the Austro-Hungarian monarchy. It is also a key principle in the United States; and it should also be a ruling principle for the EU. Very simply, subsidiarity is the principle that issues should be addressed by the lowest institutional level that is competent to resolve them, whether in countries, states, or other social institutions; higher levels of organization should never take over functions that can be handled better and more competently by lower levels. For example, cities should never take over roles that families can manage; states should not do what counties, towns, or families can do; nations should not preempt the role of states. The Europe Union bureaucracy in Brussels should not concern itself with problems that can be solved on the national level.

Subsidiarity has been a bedrock principle of Catholic social teaching for millennia. God gave each of us an intellect and a free will in order that we should take proper responsibility for our actions according to our station in life. But in addition to good theology, subsidiarity is simply sensible — and politically efficient — policy. When an institution is closer to a problem, it is usually best equipped to handle it.

Unfortunately, we are living in a time where there is a strong desire to centralize lawmaking and policymaking at higher and higher organizational levels. Institutions, and individuals, are succumbing to the ever-present temptation to expand their power and grab competencies from lower levels. Indeed, this tendency seems only to be increasing: some people would make lower levels (nations, states, townships, even families) effectively disappear in order to create worldwide structures that can address every problem.

Why is this dangerous? Several reasons. First, it is simply inefficient to have people who are far removed from a problem trying to find solutions. They simply cannot know as much about particular local conditions as the people who are closer to a problem. As a result, their solutions are unlikely to be as effective. But perhaps more concerning is the issue of accountability. When decisions about local matters are made from afar, if the decisions are poor and cause unanticipated problems, it is hard to know who is responsible and who can correct the new problems—or who must be replaced. This damages the democratic process, which is designed to choose the best leaders. Most importantly, human beings are made for local interaction, in families, towns, and countries with common cultures. That's just the way we are made. Ties above "nation"—which rely simply on a common humanity—are inevitably weak and exert such a weak claim on individuals that the force of the state (like in George Lucas' galaxy) ends up replacing love and affection as a motivating force for individuals.

So, subsidiarity is a critical idea for our times. Put the word in your pocket and use it a lot. And explain it to people if they find it complicated.

An empire built on subsidiarity

A famous and funny saying jokes that the Holy Roman Empire was neither Holy, nor Roman, nor an Empire. While the original Roman Empire had disappeared after AD 476, plunging Europe into a dark and confusing few centuries, when Charles the Great ("Charlemagne") was crowned King of the Empire in Rome by Pope Leo III in the year 800, a new overarching state structure was created that indeed comprised many of the original Roman states. In fact, by the Middle Ages, this state structure governed most of the Roman Empire's former territory, including Germany, Netherlands, Switzerland, Austria, Slovenia, Czech Republic, the territory of today's Poland, and Northern Italy. That's certainly an empire, reasonably "Roman" (at least geographically), and—because the Pope who governs Christ's Church on earth crowned the emperor— "holiness" was at least an aspiration.

But it's also true that the empire was loosely governed, primarily by constant haggling and negotiations between the emperor and the many local rulers—and especially with the princes who themselves were the Prince Electors who chose the emperor. True, the office of emperor was imbued with much sacrality and respect, but it came with no real budget and very limited real power to coerce. The emperor ruled over places that were never properly unified: there was no imperial capital; and there were no diplomats of the empire because the emperor did not speak for all. Rather, every country retained its own governments, laws, nobilities, patricians, and parliaments or diets. The emperor kept them together—as Habsburg biographer Martyn Rady puts it, "as if the king who keeps them together was only the king of each one of them."

It was an incredible balancing act, chess on three levels with a rotating board. And this is the world that the Habsburgs entered in 1273, and the game they played continuously from 1438 to 1806—the game (like for Frank Herbert's spice navigators) that literally ended up reshaping their DNA. When Rudolf became the first Habsburg King of the Romans, it was already a supranational institution. It remained so until the last days of the Austro-Hungarian Empire in 1918. Rudolf, and his successors, had to govern the countries of the dominion in a federalist manner, respecting the principle of subsidiarity; it was simply not possible to govern it otherwise. Habsburg archdukes always had to maintain an international heart, as they might well end up governing a multiplicity of nations; Habsburg archduchesses routinely learned many languages, as they might well marry a prince from another country.

Three hundred years later, after Rudolf, his successor Charles V explained to his son, Philip II, how he should govern the nations of his empire: "Each nation (you rule) must be approached with respect and dealt with differently according to the nature of its peoples." A Habsburg emperor of the early nineteenth century, Francis II, used to quip that a good empire was achieved when "all nations under it were all moderately discontented in the same way." In the words of Otto von Habsburg, the goal was to be supranational, to adapt to the different national realities while still leading them towards a common ordered goal. Because in fact, there was a foundation of unity within the diversity, something that Charles V used to call the *Orbis Europaeus Christianus*, the "European Christian Reign." While there were different nations in the empire, Christianity, the timeless idea of empire, and the person of the emperor himself were the unifying principles.

Charles himself represented this supranationality in his own person: he was first Flemish; then he became a Spanish King; finally, he was a "German Prince" when he became emperor. Furthermore, he had a traveling court and was well-acquainted with all the parts of his empire. When he abdicated on May 5, 1555, he calculated all the trips he had made during his reign as Holy Roman Emperor: nine times to Germany, six times to Spain, seven times to Italy, ten times to Brussels, four times to France, two times to England, and twice to Africa. Forty trips in all, at a time when travel was considerably more complicated, and risky, than it is today.

Naturally, the concept of supranationality and subsidiarity during Charles V's time was different than it would be later in the nineteenth, twentieth, or twenty-first centuries. Charles never would have countenanced voting or democracy. But the fundamental idea was similar: Charles wanted to understand local realities as much as possible, and he maintained close relations with the local diets to reinforce the idea that there was a contract between monarchs and subjects and that royal power was not unlimited but, at least to some degree, constrained by legal customs and privileges. Furthermore, this mode of Imperial governance did not encourage aggressive or expansive politics.

The idea of centralized government in the Habsburg lands began to advance under Maria Theresia. Under the influence of enlightenment ideas—and to fight bureaucratic inefficiencies—she began constructing a well-organized state apparatus, centered in Vienna, where all good measures would originate and then be dispersed throughout the empire. There was less need for regional assemblies or local lords if the machinery ran efficiently in a well-oiled fashion. In some ways, centralization was inspired by the Masonic idea that reason could determine the best policy, and therefore that all change could come from above and be implemented by a small, virtuous elite.[15]

Joseph II and Leopold II

In Maria Theresia's reign, the tendency towards centralization was constrained by the tradition of imperial subsidiarity. However, when her successors, particularly Joseph II, began to replace the system of federalism, problems emerged. Instead of respecting the different languages, nations, and cultural traditions in the diverse lands of the Habsburg rule, he decided to implement one centralized policy for his reign and to use one language and one administrating structure—all originating from Vienna. He tried to emulate his great idol, Frederick of Prussia. But the Habsburg lands were a hodgepodge of languages and peoples, not one nation like Prussia, so his new policies created a lot of conflict and

[15] The Hungarians would probably see this differently. In Hungary, the various wars of independence—from Bocskai, to Rákóczi, to the Wesselényi conspiracy—were seen as fights against Habsburg centralism, and they all occurred well before the time of Maria Theresia. But it was the Hungarian example that later taught the Habsburgs about the importance of subsidiarity and respecting regional identities, which are important factors in Hungarian politics even to this day.

discord. Joseph abolished local privilege, rights, and structures in Bohemia and Hungary. In fact, on April 18, 1784, he took the Hungarian sacred crown of St. Stephen from Pozsony (now Bratislava) where it was kept and brought it into the *Schatzkammer* in Vienna. He believed that since there was an emperor in Vienna, crowns were no longer needed elsewhere. He also decided that German should be the official language in all of the Habsburg lands. The Hungarians were outraged. While there was never serious resistance, there were protests, and many dreamed of throwing off the Habsburg yoke. Joseph was seen as the "king with the hat" and not the Hungarian crown.

Finally, towards the end of his ten-year reign, menaced by a near-revolt in Hungary, Joseph began to realize that he had gone too far. Just before his death in February 1790, he arranged to have the crown sent back to Hungary. But while the crown was still making its triumphant way to Buda[16] (throngs of celebrants rejoiced along the way), Joseph II died on February 20.

It is noteworthy that his brother, Leopold II, though educated according to similar rationalistic Enlightenment ideas, always had a less rigorous, dogmatic approach to governance. There are scores of letters between the two brothers in which Joseph criticized Leopold — who was, for twenty-five years, a much-loved Grand Duke — for his actions in Florence. Leopold reformed his country, but always cautiously and with the help of competent advisors. He in turn watched the actions of his brother in Vienna with critical eyes. So it is no surprise that Leopold spent the short not-even-two-years of his reign — from September 1790 to March 1792 — correcting some of his brother's excesses. In addition to trying to repair some of the damage Joseph

[16] The modern city of Budapest is really two older cities, Buda and Pest.

had inflicted on the Church, Leopold also worked hard to console the different dominions of the Habsburgs. He calmed the Hungarian diet by reestablishing Latin (rather than German) as the official language of Parliament and the bureaucracy. To ameliorate the affront caused by Joseph's removal of the crown, Leopold allowed himself to be crowned as King of Hungary in November 1790. Furthermore, he nominated his own son, Alexander, as Palatine of Hungary (an intermediary between the Hungarian diet and King) in a great sign of respect for that local institution. Finally, Leopold referred to the Estates of the Habsburg nations as "pillars of the monarchy." So without actually undermining the essence of Joseph's reforms, Leopold was able to reinvigorate the principle of subsidiarity.

This was probably fortunate, as on August 6, 1806 (to stymie Napoleon's ambitions), the Holy Roman Empire was officially ended. Francis now could exclusively look after his Habsburg lands. He "retired" to his Habsburg countries and assumed the name "Francis I" as Austrian Emperor. He took the coat-of-arms, the famous Double Eagle, which had become the symbol par excellence of the Habsburgs. But most importantly, he preserved the Habsburg legacy—and indeed, after the Napoleonic era and the turmoil that swept Europe for first several decades of the nineteenth century, the idea of empire continued in an invigorated Austria.

Franz Joseph

Franz Joseph took over the Empire in 1848, but he had much less respect for the different nations, languages, and local customs of the lands he ruled than had some of his predecessors. In a way, it is understandable: in the months preceding Ferdinand's resignation and Franz Joseph's own ascension to the throne, the capitals of Europe and of the Habsburg Empire were being burned, as nationalistic ideas transformed nations into powder kegs. The imperial family itself had to flee rather ingloriously several times. Moreover, when the legendary Chancellor and Foreign Minister Klemens von Metternich had stepped down on March 14, 1848, the Habsburg Empire was shaken and looked as if it might break apart within weeks. Franz Joseph cracked down hard and, for about ten years, established a regime that has been called neo-absolutistic. During the crisis of 1848, he had spoken favorably about the possibility of permitting a constitution; now he retracted that promise.

But more and more, he followed the vision that he had outlined in a speech when he assumed power. He had vowed to unite all the countries of the monarchy into a great state body. Even the motto he used for his reign, *Viribus Unitis* ("with united force") reflected his policy ideals. Franz Joseph balanced all the emerging national enthusiasm in each of the countries of his empire by keeping them all united under a great idea.

But two blows softened his "hardline" stance. After the defeats of Solferino (1859) and Königgrätz against the Prussians (1866), Franz Joseph finally turned to more respectful solutions. In 1867, he implemented a great reorganization of the Austro-Hungarian government by forming the "Imperial and Royal Dual Monarchy" with the two equal halves of the empire. This provided a new foundation for the peaceful coexistence of many nations under one crown. As his predecessor had done, Franz Joseph allowed himself to be crowned King of Hungary, and his wife Queen of Hungary, as a sign of respect. In the subsequent years, he created a functioning, vital state that allowed Germans, Hungarians, Czechs, Slovaks, Poles, Serbs, Croats, Ruthenes (in today's Ukraine), Romanians, Slovenes, and Italians all to live well under the same system. The system accounted for different languages in the same parliament, and pastors of every Christian church, as well as other religions, were allowed to serve in the army. The anthem *"Gott, erhalte"* ("God, maintain") was sung in each of the different languages of the empire because there was not one mandated imperial language. (To imagine the force of this policy, imagine hearing the "Marseillaise" or the "Star-Spangled Banner" sung in another language.)

Of course, while national pride is a virtue, and while the sovereignty of nations must be respected, an aggressive nationalism sometimes has a tendency to turn against neighboring states. But the most beneficial aspect of the "k.u.k. monarchy" (*kaiserlich und königlich*, because the emperor was emperor only in Austria, while king in Hungary) was that it was proved to be a counterweight to exactly that sort of aggressive nationalism.

This, by the way, may be a good indicator of the maturity of a nation: the ability to be incorporated into a supranational structure—provided that structure is based on subsidiarity and respects the nation.[17]

But even so, the empire was so large, it was hard to solve all its problems. The fact that the Slavs in many countries of the monarchy were kept out of this "dual monarchy"—and did not enjoy the

[17] It is often said that the European Union (for which Otto von Habsburg fought for decades) is the heir of the Austro-Hungarian, or even the Holy Roman, Empire. To a certain extent, that is true: many countries live together under one rule to pursue certain common aims and interests. However, I believe that the increasing political tension in Europe stems from the fact that there is no real overarching leadership that embodies traditional, European values the way the emperor, in his very person, reminded people of the things that united them. Furthermore, although the principle of subsidiarity is a part of Article 5 of the Treaty on the European Union, the current EU has a tendency to disregard subsidiarity in too many cases. The Habsburgs learned about the importance of local governance the hard way. God willing, the European Union will learn it as well.

privileges of the Germans and Hungarians—created unrest in the final decades of the monarchy. If Franz Ferdinand had not been killed in Serejevo but had become emperor in 1916 when his uncle died, perhaps he would have managed to incorporate the Slavic countries of the monarchy more fully. Contrary to what you may have read elsewhere, even the successor to the Holy Roman Empire, the Austro-Hungarian empire, was not, in its last years, a "rotten multinational state" or a "doomed construct." Prominent historians such as Timothy Snyder have demonstrated that it was a vibrant and functioning monarchy up to the very last years and months. Had the war not put an end to it, who knows how long a reformed Habsburg reign might have lasted?

In the end, the idea of empire (in German, *reich*) has shaped Europe for nearly six hundred years, with greater and lesser success. But one historical curiosity about the Holy Roman Empire is that, according to some legal scholars, it never officially, legally ended. The Principality of Liechtenstein—and the Collegio Teutonico in the Church of Santa Maria dell'Anima—are tiny pieces of the empire that continue to exist, unchanged since their formation in the eighteenth and fifteenth centuries, even after 1806 when the Holy Roman Empire ended. So, it is no surprise that if you visit the church of Santa Maria dell'Anima, you will discover a plethora of Double Eagles. So very technically speaking, the empire continues even to this day. And who knows, as Fr. Aidan Nichols once wondered, perhaps someday in the future it will once again "en-soul" a united Europe?

But, fantastic speculation aside, the often-forgotten aspect of empire that I most want to highlight is, again, subsidiarity. The Joseph II episode teaches a very important lesson for us today. Whenever higher levels of organization, removed from the issues they are confronting, impose suffocating measures in the name of an idea, an ideology, or the latest scientific fad, the tentacles of a new Enlightened Absolutism ("we know more than my subjects; we know what's good for them; and we will enforce it") are beginning to spread. And your response should be clear: remember that you are not subjects; protest like the Hungarians did under Joseph II; and demand that the principle of subsidiarity be respected.

RULE 4

STAND FOR LAW
AND JUSTICE

(and Your Subjects)

GEORGE LUCAS's *STAR WARS* is not the only fantasy that challenges the idea of empire. The foundational myth of "fighting unjust tyrants" is deeply embedded into the origin of the United States of America; it may take effort for my American readers to accommodate their thinking to the idea that the very purpose of monarchies was to stand for law, justice, and peace for your people. Monarchs may not always have achieved this goal, either internally or along their borders, but, nevertheless, it was the goal and their purpose.

Partly, it may be more difficult for Americans to understand real monarchies because they rarely encounter real royals; and they tend to have little sense of actual royalty throughout history. They haven't seen, or considered, how future monarchs were raised; how they took their first responsibilities and finally took over from their parents; how they then raised children of their own. All they imagine is an oppressive tyrant, sitting on a far-away throne. But the populations in countries with active monarchs, who witness royalty directly or are raised to consider the history of royalty throughout the generations, benefit from a completely different perspective, and this creates a close social bond. Furthermore, as a cousin to many modern royals, I personally have had the additional advantage of knowing and understanding the goals and aspirations of some of the princes and princesses who became rulers.

What did I find? I met people who, since their earliest childhood, were raised *to serve*—to serve their country with every appearance, every gesture, every parade, every photo. Just as their parents and grandparents had done before. Since they were young, they got to know their countries, the political parties and politicians, and the Church representatives. They learned about all the fault lines that menaced their country. They watched as their parents dealt with many problems. And they were told how their grandparents had confronted similar problems.

Serving always meant putting your own interests second. In a country with several languages, your preferred language was not used exclusively; rather, all the country's languages were spoken. Your preference for one region or for one kind of people could not be indulged. You were a symbol of unity and had to show respect to all regions and all people. Furthermore, you knew that any mess you created when you were eventually in the position of power would burden your children when they came to power. Finally, at least in my youth there was very little option to renounce your responsibilities and disappear into a private life. You simply owed it to your country: for God's sake, and for the many privileges you had been given. And precisely because you were not elected—and therefore not obliged to calibrate your decisions to ensure re-election—you were specially positioned to engage real problems honestly.

You may say this is a rose-tinted view. Perhaps. But nevertheless, it is what I have seen.

Even if modern European monarchies have very limited constitutional powers — indeed, they have far less power than an American president — their real power is the power of example. But that was always a critical, perhaps the most critical, role played by monarchs. Whether a monarch is upholding the law, or simply the Truth, a Catholic monarch who believes in God understands that He will, someday, render final judgment.

Contrast this mindset with some modern politicians. Not having been raised to responsibility, and with less permanently secure positions, they will quite understandably be more naturally tempted to use their careers as paths to personal advancement, profiting off the connections made during those careers. Nobody can blame them. But this was something rulers in the past need not have done.

From the first Habsburg Emperor, Rudolf in 1273, the Habsburgs defended the law, tried to be just, and tried to improve the lives of their subjects. Remember, there had been a nearly thirty-year interregnum after the fall of the House of Hohenstaufen, so there had been constant fights, conflicts, and lawlessness. Rudolf's first challenge was to restore order, which he did with remarkable success. He worked with local rulers to reorganize territories taken in those thirty years from the empire (the so-called "Revendication"). He gave them a juridical structure and abolished tolls unlawfully instituted during the interregnum. He forced his great rival Ottokar of Bohemia to give back all the countries he had taken — Central Austria, Styria, and Carinthia — that were then still independent lands. (First the lands were placed under imperial guardianship; later, when Ottokar was defeated, Rudolf gave the lands to his own sons.)

So the role of the emperors — as the "kings above kings" — required them to take law and justice very, very seriously.[18] And like their forebear Rudolf, they did. There are too many Habsburg emperors to review each of their records; but it is worth considering at least a few examples of how seriously they stood for law, justice, and their subjects:

✠ Frederick III, who was the father of Emperor Maximilian and reigned during the middle of the fifteenth century, spent most of his time as emperor debating laws in meetings. He personally worked on and contributed to fifty thousand legal documents over the years of his reign.

✠ Charles V saw his subjects in the New World not as servants to be exploited, but as subjects to be treated fairly. He once wrote that care for indigenous people was "our responsibility, for the honor of God and the sake of justice." Because he recognized in them fellow human souls, he was particularly concerned that they get to know the Faith so they could go to Heaven. (He did also refer to them as "distant Calcuttish folk," but that was not meant to be derogative — they simply thought that America was part of India.)

✠ Ferdinand I, around 1520, once conceded to his aristocratic subjects "the right to lift weapons against him if he ever touched their rights and privileges."

[18] Even if they were above kings, emperors could still be "men of the people" when needed. Once when Rudolf was traveling on a very narrow path, a peasant, who wanted to squeeze by, said grumpily: "I would squeeze by, but your huge nose is in the way!" Rudolf pushed the tip of his (indeed huge) nose to the side and said: "Now it will be possible, I believe."

✠ In the eighteenth century, Maria Theresia, of course, was famous for being the preeminent reformer of government, including the civil service, codes of law, and the entire structure of her state. Her guiding thought and deep conviction was that monarchs were appointed by God for the common welfare.

✠ Joseph II, despite the faults detailed above, believed that as an enlightened—and absolute—ruler, it was his responsibility to educate his subjects. In order to understand how to do that best, he really tried to get to know simple people, in order to hear their plight. He must have met, in person, literally millions of his subjects in the many audiences he gave as he travelled throughout his reign.[19] He also tried to end the system of serfdom. And he gave religious tolerance

[19] A nice anecdote about one of these encounters shows how he was "a people's man" at a time that other royals were not:

Once when he was traveling anonymously in his carriage, Joseph II came upon another carriage that had gone to pieces beside the road. He offered the stranded traveler a place in his own carriage. Rolling through the countryside, the traveler jokingly asked the emperor to guess what he had eaten for lunch. The emperor proposed everything from chicken fricassee to an omelet, but couldn't guess it. "I ate roast veal," he said with a laugh, slapping the emperor's leg.

Joseph countered: "We don't know each other, so now it's your time to guess: Who am I?" The man replied: "A soldier?" "Perhaps, but I might be more," said the emperor. "You look young for an officer," the man continued, but then guessed higher and higher ranks: "Are you a colonel? A major? A governor?" "No," came the answer every time. "Don't tell me you're the emperor," the man finally gasped incredulously. "You guessed it," exclaimed Joseph, and heartily slapped the man's leg.

The man, horrified, wanted to leave the carriage because he had slapped the emperor's leg. "No, no, no," the emperor said gently. "Nothing has changed. I knew who I was, you didn't. Let's roll on."

to all groups (except, as we saw, to "useless" Catholic contemplative orders).

✠ Leopold, Joseph's brother, went so far as to say once that the monarch was accountable not only to God, but to his people: "Princes must always be conscious ... that they owe their position only to an agreement between other men; that they in turn must perform their duties and tasks, as rightly expected of them. ... Princes must always remember that they cannot degrade other men without degrading themselves."

✠ Leopold's ten sons — the young archdukes Francis, Ferdinand, Charles, Alexander, Joseph, Anton, John, Rainer, Louis, and Rudolf — were all given a brilliant education in Florence. They read the classics from Caesar to the most recent radical French philosophers. Locke and Rousseau were a normal part of their formation — as was praying the rosary, on the insistence of Grandmother Maria Theresia. Whenever a famous professor or artist passed through town, he was summoned to the Palazzo Pitti where he taught the princes — or sometimes followed their classes, to observe how the princes were being educated. The princes were also trained to be able to do work with their hands; their father wanted his sons to grow up humble, dutiful, and devoted to the well-being of their subjects. And when those archdukes (whom I like to refer to as the "glorious generation") were let out into the world, they did everything they could to improve the lives of the monarchy's subjects. (One day, perhaps, I will write a book about that group; it wasn't always easy for Francis to be surrounded by such brilliant brothers who constantly peppered him with their great ideas.)

Francis became a reform-minded emperor. His younger brother Ferdinand continued the work of reform in Tuscany that his father had begun. Another brother, Charles, became a great general—perhaps the greatest the family ever had—and fought throughout his service for the reform of the army. (At Aspern, near Vienna, he was also the first man to beat Napoleon in a land battle.) Their brother Anton Victor lived a life of service as the Grand Master of the Teutonic Order and a Bishop. Another brother, John, was perhaps the first "green" Habsburg; he promoted sustainable agriculture and foresting, before briefly becoming the first German *Reichsverweser* (an elected ruler) in 1848.

But after all these examples, it is worth further highlighting the life of their brother, Archduke Palatine Joseph of Hungary, as his life of service was particularly notable. He went to Hungary in the 1790s, and it is there that we see his passion for law-making and the defense of his subjects' welfare really take shape. (Disclaimer: he is my great-great-great grandfather, and also the founder of my Hungarian branch of the Habsburgs, so forgive me if I am enthusiastic about his accomplishments.)

Joseph was a twenty-year-old lad, well-educated and with a passionate heart, when he first arrived in Hungary as governor. Francis sent Joseph with the explicit instruction "that your first duty is justice to your people." After much pleading, Joseph was made Palatine—the office responsible for communication between the Hungarians and their king in Vienna, Joseph's brother Francis—and he took his responsibilities for Hungarian interest very much to heart. (Joseph once said, of his own loyalties: "The emperor is my brother; but if he should violate the least of your rights, I would forget the ties of blood to remind myself that I am your Palatine.")

In fact, Joseph had fallen in love with this unique, proud, and splendid people (who were seen mostly as a nuisance in Vienna) even before he had arrived in Hungary. He had taken the step of learning Hungarian law from a leading canon lawyer, and it was he who had convinced his brother to allow the Hungarians to call in the diet, first in 1796, then in 1801. (This took some doing, but Vienna was under pressure because it needed Hungarian conscripts in the fight against Napoleon. Joseph played that card to get more concessions for the Hungarians.) Joseph even got his brother Francis—who was not a particularly attractive man—to pose for a painting, wearing the Hungarian hussar uniform, as a strong sign of respect for the Hungarians. For once in his life, Francis looked positively magnificent.

Joseph worked tirelessly in the diet. Occasionally he became impatient with the institutional suspicion and stubbornness, both on the Hungarian side and on the side of Francis and his ministers. Over the next fifty years, he became the leading advocate to bring this part of the empire into the nineteenth century as he reformed laws, built up civic institutions (like firefighters and public schools), facilitated construction of railroads, instituted the Academy for sciences, and served the people of Hungary up to his death in 1847, on the eve of the 1848 revolution.

Some today might accuse Joseph of having "gone native." Nevertheless, in Budapest there is still a square with a beautiful statue dedicated to him: *József Nádor tér*, *"Joseph Anton square."*[20] In the *Sándor Palota*, the Hungarian President's Palace on the Castle Hill, in the central chamber, you can see a huge portrait of the Palatine, in his magnificent hussar uniform, sporting his magnificent mustache. (Also depicted are some of the things he seems to be most proud of, the four volumes of the *Acta Dietalia*, the documentation of sessions in the diet for which he worked so hard.)

[20] His full name was Joseph Anton John the Baptist of Austria.

In Archduke Palatine Joseph's life, many of the elements of the "Habsburg Way" worked well together, particularly his combined commitment to the empire and subsidiarity. The complicated relationship between the court in Vienna and the Hungarians was always a dance between centralism and subsidiarity. Joseph played a key role in maintaining this balance. But his efforts to give more power to local institutions were most noteworthy.

After Joseph's death, his son Stephen (who was the last palatine) stood side-by-side with the Hungarians in the revolution of 1848. He and the entire branch of Hungarian Habsburgs saw themselves as Hungarians first. But the Hungarian demands that he brought to Vienna were seen as a threat to the unity of the empire. When the Hungarians declared that the Viennese Habsburgs had forfeited their throne, the Hungarian fight for freedom was brutally suppressed, with the help of the armies of the Russian Czar.

For ten years, centralism dominated the first period of Emperor Franz Joseph's rule. Finally, through the intercession of Franz Joseph's wife, Empress Elisabeth, the autonomy of Hungary that had been restricted since 1848 was restored in the Austro-Hungarian Compromise of 1867.

There is much more to be said about the "glorious generation" of Francis and his brothers, especially about their modesty and frugality. But I want to finish with an amusing anecdote that illustrates what was typically said of them. When the poet Byron spent his famous summer on Lake Geneva in 1816 with Mary Wollstonecraft and her lover Percy B. Shelley, a literary bet prompted Mary to create the first scene of what was to become her immortal novel *Frankenstein*. During the same stay, Byron himself wrote a fragmentary novel, and his personal physician, John William Polidori, also wrote *The Vampyre*, the precursor of romantic vampire stories. However, Byron and Polidori had a falling out, and so Polidori left on a trip to Italy. Coming from Switzerland, Polidori crossed over the Grand St. Bernard and spent the night of September 27, 1816, in the monastery located at the top of the mountain pass. He notes in his diary that there was great excitement there: another simple traveler had stayed the previous night, and the monks had only just discovered, through his signature in the monk's guest book, that the guest had been the famous Archduke Rainer, Viceroy of Lombardo-Venetia. Rainer, one of the "glorious brothers," is known to regularly have hiked, incognito, along the borders of his reign, in order to better understand his subjects (and to study rock formations).

Finally, I want to end the chapter with an anecdote about Franz Joseph standing up for his subjects. In 1910, the old emperor met with the former president of the United States, Theodore Roosevelt, in the Hofburg. When the former president and Noble Peace Prize winner asked the emperor to explain to him exactly what he was doing—implying, I suspect, that elected parliaments and governments had made the emperor's role a superfluous anachronism—the emperor answered simply: "The idea of my office is to protect my peoples from their politicians."

I leave you with this question: Who protects the voters from their politicians today?

RULE 5

KNOW WHO
YOU ARE

(and Live Accordingly)

My Uncle Otto von Habsburg, the son of the last emperor (and famously depicted in a photograph standing beside the old emperor as a blonde-locked young boy), was a brilliant orator. I heard him speak several times at political events, holding large audiences captive as he reflected on European values — and some Habsburg values, too. One of his signature lines was: "Those who don't know where they come from do not know where they are heading — because they don't know where they stand."

On one level, this is simply an invitation to study history. As Winston Churchill said, "Those that fail to learn from history are doomed to repeat it."[21] But on a deeper level, this maxim applies to individuals and families about themselves. Indeed, the entire Habsburg family has always been keenly aware of its deep roots, what shaped it, and where it came from. Although mostly the Habsburgs were deeply traditional people, that didn't keep them from innovating, when necessary. We are all swept, whether we

[21] Churchill was paraphrasing Spanish philosopher George Santayana who said: "Those who cannot remember the past are condemned to repeat it."

like it or not, into the future, every moment of our lives. When you "know yourself," you can carry yourself into the future without losing yourself along the way.[22]

Habsburg myth-building

As we've seen, we know pretty well where the Habsburgs come from geographically—remember, they appeared somewhere between the Alsace and Switzerland and sometime before the year 950. For a single family (or even for a state), that is a very long time ago. But as we saw in the family history and the story of the empire, shortly after the Habsburgs were catapulted from their minor position as Swiss counts to the highest office—King of the Holy Roman Empire—they lost this high standing again. From the death of Rudolf I in 1291, the Habsburgs were on the sidelines as the Prince Electors from other noble houses did everything they could to keep the Swiss-Austrian parvenus out of the game. The Golden Bull of 1356 did not even mention them as electors, which was quite a blow to Rudolf IV ("The Founder"), who was not only building himself a university and a cathedral in Vienna, but also did everything else he could to impress his father-in-law, the emperor, in order to get his family back into the Imperial limelight.

Rudolf IV and Archdukes

In addition to politicking, the Habsburgs used their own more creative means to enhance their political standing. First, this was the moment when, having ruled Austria for seventy-five years, they

---

[22] The Greek aphorism γνῶθι σεαυτόν (transliterated: *gnōthi seauton*) means "know yourself."

begin to drop the title "Count of Habsburg" in favor of the more elegant "House of Austria."

Then, funnily enough, two years after the Golden Bull, it just so happened that Rudolf IV managed to discover a very interesting series of documents in his archives that, until then, had been curiously overlooked. It contained, among others, a letter. From Julius Caesar. Julius, it seemed, had written to the Austrians exhorting them to obey none other than the *Comes Austriae*, Caesar's own uncle. It began as follows:

"We, Emperor Julius, Caesar and Worshipper of the Gods, Supreme Augustus, Strengthener of the whole universe, to Austria and its people, the Grace of Rome and our peace." And then the document specified that this great *Comes Austriae*, his uncle and a senator, should always be obeyed—and furthermore, that the land should be his fief, forever. You have guessed, of course, that this senator was an ancestor of the Habsburgs.

No less astonishingly, among the documents there was another one that was ostensibly written by the Emperor Nero, which allowed the Habsburgs, thenceforth, to use the title "Archduke." Suddenly, they were lifted to almost the same rank as the Prince Electors themselves!

The collection of documents, which are today known as the *Privilegium Maius*, are composed in a flowery style of Latin that a rather bombastic pupil (or ambitious count) might have used. They also contain factual errors. Not surprisingly, when the emperor was asked to ratify these documents, his advisor, the famous humanist Petrarch, deemed them clumsy forgeries. Nevertheless, the Habsburgs began using the title archduke, and the title is still used to this day. Why? Because in 1453, a hundred years later, a Habsburg was again emperor. Of course he authenticated the document. At which point, as they say, that was that. Whatever their murky origins, the moment the documents were recognized as authentic by the emperor they had the force of imperial law.

Frederick and AEIOU

Speaking of Emperor Frederick III, you may recall that under his reign and the reign of his son, Maximilian ("The Last Knight"), the fate of the Habsburgs changed. Perhaps this was because Frederick, who was in some ways a quiet, phlegmatic man, also dreamed big as he spent much of his life in provincial Wiener Neustadt south of Vienna. He was interested in old genealogies, mystical mottos, and even astrology. In 1437, when Frederick was particularly concerned about his finances and his power, he made a rather dramatic motto for himself with the five vowels, the enigmatic abbreviation AEIOU. He put the motto on documents, images, even his buildings. (You can still see it on his monumental sarcophagus in Vienna's Stephansdome, and many other places as well.)[23]

What was the meaning of this motto? It is still debated. Most historians favor the interpretation: *Austriae Est Imperare Orbi Universo* (or *Austria Est Imperator Orbis Universi*). Roughly translated, this means "Austria should be ruling all the earth" (or "is ruling," as eventually became the case). But others interpret it to mean: *Aquila Electa Iuste Omnia Unicat* ("The elected Eagle rightly unifies everything"). And German-speaking citizens read it as *Aller Ehren Ist Oesterreich Voll* ("Austria is full of all honors"). In fact, there are dozens of suppositions.

In any case, Frederick was deeply convinced of the power of royal blood. He was confident that the Habsburgs would really

[23] By the way, this sarcophagus really contains the remains of Frederick and has been opened in recent times.

rule the world, someday. In the 1430s, this was an absolute absurdity. But when Frederick died in 1493, the empire was in fact becoming a world power. What do they always say in the movies, believe in yourself and you can make your dreams come true? Frederick lived his dream.

Frederick was also concerned about conquering the past. He delved deeply into genealogy (as many other rulers did at the time) and was strongly inspired by a fanciful genealogy book of the time, the so-called *Chronicle of the Ninety-Five Lords*. He developed a genealogy that traced the Habsburg family all the way back to the time of Augustus, and even to the rulers of Troy.

Maximilian and genealogy

I have already spoken about the magnificent character of Emperor Maximilian, Frederick's son, and how he expanded the Habsburg reign worldwide. But he also had a romantic, fanciful side. Not only was he still jousting in knightly tournaments long after the age of chivalry had ended (hence his epithet, "The Last Knight"), but he also wrote three colorful autobiographies that catalogued — and romanticized — three phases of his own life, recounting exhilarating adventures full of traps, cunning, enemies, and daring feats. Amusingly, the protagonist himself is often portrayed as a bit of a dunce who was often unable to recognize how evil his so-called advisors were. But of course, he still prevails against his foes, due to his great strength and fantastic abilities.

Maximilian also loved genealogies. He managed to produce family back even further than Troy. In fact, his genealogy — which he compelled the Theological faculty of Vienna to construct — showed a descent all the way back from Noah in the Bible. (Before that, it didn't matter because every human being descended from Adam and Eve.) But Noah was quite an ancestor to have!

Maximilian's love for genealogy can be seen today in the *Habsburgersaal* ("Habsburg hall") in the Tratzberg Castle in Austria.[24] The owners of the castle dedicated one entire room to the descent of the Habsburgs as a present to Maximilian, who regularly visited them. Standing in this room is quite overwhelming. Beginning over the entrance door with Rudolf I (fancifully killing Ottokar of Bohemia himself with a sword in the Battle of Dürnkrut, which he never did), portraits of Habsburgs go all along the left wall of the room, connected by the branches of a curling, twisting, family tree. On the right-hand side, you finally find Maximilian himself, his two children by Mary of Burgundy — and, near the door, a contour of his future grandchild, Charles V, whom Juana was expecting at the time.

The Habsburg family tree at that time was less than three hundred years old (not counting the descent from Noah), but it was enough to give Maximilian immense pride. Imagine if he had known that, four hundred years later, his family would still be ruling. Or that five hundred years later, it would still be thriving.

While the genealogical creativity exercised by some of the early Habsburgs with respect to their family's past may have been a bit fanciful, their hopes for the future were indeed fulfilled. At least partly, this was because they knew about the importance of having a vision about yourself. They understood that having an idea of where you came from would play an important role in determining where you went. And who knows: perhaps their lofty vision of the past — precisely because it was wishful — helped make their future wishes come true.

[24] You can also go to YouTube and watch a short clip of this author explaining it.

The Golden Fleece

Another element of the Habsburg family lore entered the family with Emperor Maximilian. When he married Mary of Burgundy, Maximilian became the Sovereignof the Order of the Golden Fleece.

The chivalric Order of the Golden Fleece had been founded in Burgundy by Mary's grandfather Philip the Good in 1430. Over the years, it became the most prestigious order of chivalry in the world. Originally, it was probably founded to bind "jobless" knights of the Burgundian rule closer to Duke Philip and to help unify his territories, which spanned from the North Sea almost to the Alps. But it became the highest of honors.

The Order is deeply imbued with Catholic symbolism. Knights of the Order promise to uphold the Catholic faith and to defend Our Lady, the Church, and the poor. They swear all of this, even to this day, in front of a richly decorated Oath Cross that contains a splinter of the True Cross of Christ. The feast day of the Order is November 30, which is the Feast of St. Andrew. It is on that day that new knights are initiated into the Order.

Very few symbols are as strongly connected with the Habsburg family as the golden, stylized symbol of a hanging sheep skin, fashioned after the legend of Jason and the Argonauts. You will find it dangling from the necks of hundreds and hundreds of Habsburgs over the centuries. In fact, when you notice this decoration on a painting, it is usually because you have a Habsburg in front of you, or a close ally of the Habsburg rulers.

The members of the Order are all male, Catholic, and from the aristocracy—and there are never more than fifty. The decorations are the huge collars (kept in safes and only worn for two Holy Masses at the Feast of the Order), the classical neck decoration (worn with "white tie"), and a smaller buttonhole-version that knights wear at solemn occasions. For most of knights, there is also a tiny version that we wear on our body all the time, usually on a necklace, beside the cross or a medal of Our Lady. A knight never forgets that he is a Knight of the Golden Fleece.

Habsburgs do not get the Fleece automatically, as they once did for their eighteenth birthday. Now, no more than fifteen of the knights are members of the Habsburg family. As a knight and diplomat to the Holy See, I am fortunate to be able to wear the neck decoration regularly as a tailcoat (white tie, but with a black vest) is our "working outfit" when we attend solemn Masses in St. Peter's Basilica.

I should add that, after the end of the Habsburg rule in Spain, the Spanish kings claimed the Golden Fleece for themselves, so the decorations of the Order can be seen in Spain, too. In Spain it is not a strict, knightly order but is given out by the king as an award of the state. Women and non-Catholics are both eligible. But to this day, the Austrian Golden Fleece is given to only a handful of new knights each year, by the head of our family (and Sovereign of the Order), so it is a great honor.

"Spanish" court ceremonial

There is one more Habsburg family tradition that has helped to define who we are: the famous Spanish court ceremonial that, up until the last decades of the Habsburg history, organized life at court. The "Sisi" movies with Romy Schneider provide a sense of the ceremony, and it is easy to sympathize with the young empress who rebels against the stiff court protocol, enforced by the imposing mother of Emperor Franz Joseph, the Archduchess Sophie (with her arched eyebrow). While the "Spanish" protocol was no longer fully observed in 1853, the courtly traditions of that day were derived from it.

Interestingly, the Spanish ceremonial was not Spanish at all. It was actually imported from Burgundy and had been developed by Philip the Good at the same time as the creation of the Golden Fleece. It was a very detailed set of social rules that he used to help bind his diverse lands together. Brought to Spain by Maximilian's grandson Charles V, it dominated Habsburg court life for the next centuries, both in Spain and in Austria. Under Joseph II, it was (of course) reduced sharply, and indeed practically abolished. But it was still practiced until the 1960s in almost its original form in the Papal court and later in the Vatican.

One story from 1740 shows how deeply the Habsburgs were influenced by the court protocol. When the father of Maria Theresia, Charles VI, lay dying, he desperately tried to speak. When he was finally able to breathe out a few words, he whispered "Eight candles!" At the foot of his bed, there were only four candles burning. Protocol foresaw that a dying Holy Roman Emperor was entitled to eight candles!

While the requirements of protocol may seem stifling at times, serving in Rome as a diplomat has made me appreciate its importance. Even if the protocol used today at the Holy See is a pale reminder of something that was once extremely rigid, it nevertheless facilitates relations between states. Protocol sets a table for the diplomatic game because it provides a common space and a set of common rules for meaningful encounters. In fact, I believe that protocol itself is the very thing that keeps diplomacy alive in a time of great chaos. It protects the weak from the strong and promotes dialogue even — and especially — when words fail.

Let me just mention one other "Spanish" element that remained visible in Austria: the two Pillars of Hercules. This was a symbol of Charles V, a reference to the Strait of Gibraltar, and a reminder that the Habsburg Empire reached across all the known seas. (*Plus Ultra,*

"Further Beyond," was Charles's motto.) The Pillars of Hercules can be seen in many paintings and sculptures, but they are most visible in front of the *Karlskirche*. When Maria Theresia's father, Charles VI, built that church, he demonstrated his connection to his Spanish heritage—and his great predecessor, Charles V—by erecting these two columns. Of course, the other place where you can still find this symbol today is on the coat of arms of Spain.

Speaking of coats of arms, I should mention the Double Eagle here. The eagle with two heads is a very old symbol that existed even in Babylonian times. However, as a coat of arms, it was first the symbol of the Holy Roman Empire, but then increasingly stood for the Habsburg family itself. In fact, after the end of the Holy Roman Empire in 1806, the Habsburgs took the symbol with them into the Austro-Hungarian Monarchy. Is it found wherever the Habsburgs went.[25]

Though the depictions varied over the centuries, on a typical Habsburg double eagle coat of arms, you will usually see the red-white-red field (originally for Austria, but in this context the House of Austria), a red lion with a blue crown (the oldest Habsburg crest), and, in later times—you will know why, if you have paid attention—a diagonal field with three small birds inside, which is the crest of Lorraine.

Traditional Habsburgs

So, these are some of the most important achievements and traditions that define the Habsburgs: the Habsburgs' influence spread over the

---

[25] A famous book about the period after the Austro-Hungarian monarchy is titled *Was Blieb Vom Doppeladler (What Remained of The Double Eagle)*—and I myself wrote an (adorable!) children's book about "Dubbie, the double eagle." If you want to learn more about the symbol, do find a copy.

entire world; there are two branches in Spain and Austria; there was the constant re-election of a Habsburg ruler as Emperor of the Holy Roman Empire; the ancient family tree; the Order of the Golden Fleece; the Spanish Court Ceremonial; the Double Eagle.

With these things in mind, each young archduke and archduchess knew (and knows) where they came from, what they stood for, "who they were." They submitted to marriage politics and followed the Catholic faith. Even Habsburgs who, in their hearts, might not have been truly devout always remained Catholic (and indeed, required it of their subjects).

The Habsburgs were slow to change, stood for continuity and traditional values, and (with the exception of Joseph II) stand for the values of their fathers as a matter of honor.

And I think this was—and is—a very good thing.

Let us end this chapter with an amusing anecdote that shows the Habsburg spirit. In the early nineteenth century, at a time when every nation dreamed of having a Constitution like the United States, Emperor Francis II's personal doctor once remarked to him, as he was recovering from an illness: "Your Majesty must have a very good constitution [meaning, a robust health]." The emperor looked at him sharply and said: "You must change your formulations, my dear, because I don't have a constitution and never will have one!"

Francis II knew who he was and where he had come from. Can we say the same for our current political leaders? Do they know where they—or their countries—come from? Do they stand for traditional values like family and faith—or value the culture and history of their own nations? Or do they try to impose globalist ideas on countries with fundamentally different values?

Finally: what about you? Do you know who you are? Do you know the values that shaped you? Do you live accordingly? I hope so. Knowing who you are gives you sovereignty over yourself. It will give you the confidence not to be swayed by fleeting fads, but to follow the truth—about yourself and about God. The alternative is the empty aimlessness that torments so many and characterizes so much of modern life.

RULE 6

Be Brave in Battle

(or Have a Great General)

WAIT A MINUTE, you will say. Be brave in battle? Weren't the Habsburgs international, peace-loving folk who settled their problems with arranged marriages so that they never had to do battle? And weren't they too poor to afford good armies anyway?

Alas, human conflict is as old as Cain and Abel, and wars are as old as mankind. There will always be fighting, in one form or another. While Habsburg Emperors, for the most part, avoided waging wars personally, wars nevertheless still happened. When they did, there were two kinds of Habsburgs: those who were on the battlefield themselves and those who were fortunate enough to have able generals to do their work. We shall see some instances of both types.

Rudolf I

Until quite recently, being a good diplomat or administrator was almost never enough to be a good king. In fact, throughout most of human history, good kings had to be able to wield a weapon, do battle, and fight physically—and personally—for their ideas and their allies. Sometimes even to the death. Rulers were always soldiers. Consider Rudolf von Habsburg. When, in 1273, he learned that the electors had chosen him to be "King of the Romans," he was on a war campaign laying siege to the Bishop of Basel. When he heard the news, he made his peace with the bishop and left to accept his election.

Of course, martial expertise, particularly for emperors, was never limited to physical prowess. Strategic and tactical cunning were always integral parts of war as well. When Rudolf was laying siege to Vienna (probably in his long campaign against Ottokar of Bohemia), he threatened to cut off all their supplies if they didn't surrender. When the Viennese responded "Never," he let his eyes roam across the lush vineyards decorating the hills around Vienna and said, "If you don't open the gates, I will destroy your vineyards." The Viennese surrendered immediately.

But Rudolf's greatest military triumph occurred when he challenged Ottokar, on a hot day in August 1278, in the village of Dürnkrut, northeast of Vienna. Rudolf had tried everything he could think of—from peace agreements to the offer of his children in marriage—to persuade Ottokar diplomatically to return the lands he had appropriated. Finally, Rudolf decided to use his army to make his argument. He faced off against Ottokar on the plain of the Marchfeld.

Rudolf had only 4,500 knights to Ottokar's 6,500, so nominally it looked as if the day would go to the Přemysl ruler. (In addition, Ottokar's knights were more heavily armored than Rudolf's.) However, Rudolf was aware of his disadvantage, so he allied himself with the Hungarian king, László IV, who sent four thousand lightly armored Hungarians to the battle. Crucially, Rudolf kept them hidden from sight behind a hill, thereby ignoring the accepted ("fair play") practice of displaying all his knights in plain view. Rudolf then instructed a small group of trusted friends, commanded by Ulrich von Kappeln, to conduct a surprise attack on Ottokar's flank. Kappeln had to be convinced — and he almost refused. Indeed, it is said that some of Rudolf's other allies abandoned him for what they considered to be cheating.

The last great knightly battle of the Middle Ages was long and brutal. In the thick of the battle, Rudolf's horse was killed under him, but, in the end, it was the hidden reserves that decided the day. Ottokar was killed. The fleeing Bohemians were massacred by Rudolf's armies. Rudolf had won the day, even if he had failed to observe the accepted military norms.

As an Emperor, Rudolf became famous for making peace and reestablishing the law, but he was still able to get his hands dirty in a battle, when needed. And that was the dominant pattern over the next centuries.

Maximilian

For example, in the fifteenth century Emperor Maximilian had to do battle against the French to defend the Dukedom of Burgundy, which he had acquired by marrying the beautiful (and rich) Mary of Burgundy. Maximilian, as we have seen, was a passionate knight in an era when knights were all but extinct. His great military moment was the Battle of Guinegate in the Picardie in France, on August 17, 1479. Though young twenty-year-old Maximilian had dreamt of knightly battles, he had also observed that knightly armies could be beaten by soldiers on foot using pikes and long lances. (This is how the Swiss had triumphed over Charles the Bold.) Encouraged by his ally, the Count of Romont, who had witnessed the Swiss victories, Maximilian decided not only to lead his armies into battle at Guinegate, but to do so on foot inside a group of mercenary lansquenets, lance in hand. He fought with incredible courage and, after four hours, carried the field.

Lepanto

While the battles fought by Maximilian were critical for his own empire, there were other battles that were pivotal for all of Western civilization—and indeed impacted the fate of Christianity itself. When the Muslim Ottoman empire threatened the West in the sixteenth and seventeenth centuries, two critical battles were fought, Lepanto in 1571 and Vienna in 1683, and two Habsburgs played significant roles in each.

The two heroes could not have been more different. Don Juan of Austria was an illegitimate son of Emperor Charles V. He was conceived in Regensburg and raised unaware of his descent (though the old emperor acknowledged him as a son in his will). Don Juan was a passionate soldier from a young age and demonstrated his talent for war as the commander of the Spanish fleet in the Mediterranean and in battles against the moors in Andalusia. Philip II introduced the young man to court.

After the violent seizure of Cyprus by the Turks, Pope Pius V tried to arrange an alliance to put a stop to the Ottoman superiority in the Mediterranean. But intra-European politics—mostly due to the Catholic-Protestant divide—made a number of Christian rulers unenthusiastic about the Pope's plan, and many didn't want to participate. France had actually financed the Turks in order to inflict harm on the Holy Roman Empire. And even Emperor Maximilian II was reluctant to participate in the so-called Holy League so as not to estrange his Protestant princes. In the end, the alliance was comprised mostly of the Papal Fleet, Spain, Venice, and a number of Italian dukedoms and cities.

The battle occurred on October 7, 1571, in a bay off of Greece. It was the largest naval battle since antiquity, with five hundred warships involved—three hundred Turkish and two hundred Christian. Eighty thousand Christian soldiers had fasted for three days and gone to Confession and Holy Mass. They were forbidden to swear, under penalty of punishment. Rosaries in one hand, swords in the other, they sailed into battle.

It was a day of intense fighting, essentially an infantry war on floating ship-platforms. The Flagship of Don Juan, La Real, carried an image of Our Lady of Guadalupe that had been touched to the original. Whenever the outcome of the battle looked precarious, the Admiral himself prayed in front of it. At one point, the battle raged aboard La Real, and Don Juan was wounded in the melee by the Janissaries, the elite troops of the Sultan.

Finally, after five and a half hours, the day was won. Thirty thousand Ottomans and eight thousand Holy League soldiers and sailors perished. (Twelve thousand Christian rowing slaves were liberated from the Ottoman ships.)

Lepanto was a huge military victory. It also marked the beginning of the end for Ottoman expansion, at least in the Mediterranean. The final battle occurred about a hundred years later, before the gates of Vienna.

Vienna 1683

While Lepanto had destroyed the Turkish threat in the Mediterranean Sea, on land the situation remained precarious. Since the Battle of Mohács, in 1526, the Ottomans had controlled large parts of Hungary. They were even allied with rebellious Hungarian forces, who had been promised Vienna, if it could ever be taken. In 1682, the Ottoman army mobilized to march against the West.

Leopold I was an entirely different personality than his Spanish relative Don Juan of Austria. Not only was he the Emperor of the Holy Roman Empire, whose life could not be risked—even for a heroic death on the battlefield—but by the seventeeth century emperors were no longer expected to lead their forces personally into battle. However, Leopold knew what he had to do to defend his realm. War was declared on the empire on August 6, 1682, but the Turks could not begin their campaign that late in the year without the risk that winter would begin before their anticipated siege of Vienna had succeeded. The Holy Roman Empire had a year to prepare, and Leopold went to work. He formed an alliance with Venice and the Pope, which was only to be expected. But in a master stroke, he arranged the Treaty of Warsaw of 1683 in which Poland and Austria mutually promised to defend each other, if the Turks attacked either Warsaw or Vienna.

When Grand Vizier Kara Mustafa finally arrived with a huge force in Vienna on July 14, 1683, the imperial troops fled, leaving Vienna with a paltry fifteen thousand soldiers against one hundred fifty thousand Ottomans. The siege lasted two months, during which time Vienna was completely surrounded by a sea of armies. Food supplies ran low, and the Ottoman miners worked hard to dig tunnels under the walls and fortifications of the town. But on September 6, heroic Polish King Jan Sobieski crossed the Danube and met up with the imperial army, as well as allies from Saxony, Bavaria, and other countries. (Like at Lepanto, France was again conspicuously absent as it was busy taking Lorraine away from the emperor.)

Sobieski took command of eighty thousand men and, at the gates of Vienna, faced the one hundred fifty thousand Ottomans on September 12, 1683. It was just in time: the defenses were giving way and the Turks were finally breaking through at the Burg, ready to carry the fight into the inner city. But the warriors from the Holy League signaled their arrival from the heights of the *Kahlenberg*, and a Holy Mass was celebrated by Bl. Marco d'Aviano, capuchin Friar and advisor to Leopold I. Jan Sobieski served at the altar.

The battle began at four in the morning and raged throughout the entire day. Finally, King Jan Sobieski and eighteen thousand horsemen—three Polish groups and one of the Holy Roman Empire—galloped down the field in the greatest cavalry charge in history. The charge broke the Ottoman lines and the battle was won.

Although the emperor himself was not present in battle for Vienna, everyone understood that it had been his strategic maneuvering that had enabled the victory. This earned him the moniker *Türkenpoldl* ("Poldi of the Turks"—"Poldi" being an endearing abbreviation of "Leopold"). In addition, the battle signified the beginning of the end for the Turks in Europe. In the following years, Leopold I and the Holy Roman Empire—under Prince Elector Max Emmanuel and the brilliant general, Prince Eugen of Savoy—were finally able to push the Ottomans out of Hungary and farther back into the Balkans.

I would also like to give an honorary mention to Empress Maria Theresia. Throughout the early years of her reign in the 1740s, the empire was constantly at war. She famously said: "I would have been present on the battlefields against Frederick of Prussia personally—if I hadn't been pregnant or giving birth to children all the time." And in fact, as we saw, her primary battle was to re-establish the future of the Habsburg family. (With sixteen births in nineteen years of marriage, a courageous and painful effort it was.) Nevertheless, it was her brilliant success at securing military assistance from the Hungarians that saved the Habsburg empire in the very first two years of her reign—and that was critically important to the family's future as well. (While she lost the three Silesian Wars against Frederick of Prussia, her reign was able to survive these events.)

Archduke Charles and Napoleon

Perhaps not surprisingly, it is at the time of the Napoleonic Wars that we find one of the greatest Habsburg warriors, Archduke Charles of Austria. A member of the "glorious generation" of the children of Leopold II, Charles was a brilliant general and a very gifted reformer of the Austrian army. He was also a gentle husband and loving father. But he understood that fighting was sometimes necessary to protect the country, and the people, that you love. He was raised in Tuscany and later lived in the Austrian Netherlands. He saw his first battles in 1792 (when he was barely twenty) in the wars that were precipitated by the French Revolution. Immediately distinguishing himself through his courage and leadership ability, only four years later, he was seen as one of the greatest generals of Europe. He was immensely frustrated by the old-fashioned way the Austrian army was structured and commanded. He harangued his increasingly irritated brother, the emperor, with memorandums of proposed improvements.

By 1806 he was the only Austrian general who had been able to beat the French in battle, so Francis II named him Commander-in-Chief of the Austrian army and Head of his Council of War. He immediately instituted military reforms mirroring the brilliant modernizations that Napoleon had made to the French army, thus preparing them for their greatest moment: the Battle of Aspern.

The battle occurred on May 21 and 22, 1809. Napoleon was in possession of Vienna. But he had to cross the Danube in order to continue his campaign. All the bridges had been destroyed, so the French tried to cross the river north of the city, near where Nussdorf is today. Napoleon's army was repulsed, suffering a loss of seven hundred men. On May 20, Napoleon organized a second crossing attempt, by floating bridges across the Danube towards the island of Lobau, immediately south of Vienna.[26] Early on May

---

[26] Both crossing sites are today well within the modern city borders. Furthermore, because of man-made alterations to the flow of the Danube, the island of Lobau is no longer an island.

21, between the villages of Aspern and Essling, Napoleon and about twenty-five thousand of his soldiers faced ninety thousand Austrian soldiers commanded by Archduke Charles. Like his ancestor Rudolf, Charles had ordered his troops to keep themselves hidden—and allow the French to cross. When the smaller force of French realized they were facing the full Austrian army, it must have come as a complete shock. However, new French troops crossed the Danube throughout the day and the night so that, in the end, the French force inched closer and closer to eighty thousand. Nearly even.

The first day saw fierce fighting around both villages, even as the French numbers were constantly growing. Losses on both sides were horrible, and the church of Aspern was set ablaze (as is depicted in many paintings). Charles personally led a charge with the regiment flag in to Aspern village, and it was a miracle he wasn't wounded. When night fell, both armies slept within pistol shot distance of each other. But Austrian morale was high. They had survived a day against Napoleon's French army. And the new training they had been given through the efforts of the Archduke was proving its value.

The next morning, May 22, fighting resumed. The French position had improved significantly. Most of the French force had been able to cross during the night, and they were finally able to capture Aspern from the Austrians. The Austrians, meanwhile, were attacking Essling. The French pushed back strongly, and then Napoleon attacked the center of the Austrian line. The entire French front moved forward, and the Austrian line broke. Napoleon's victory seemed assured.

But then came the moment for which Archduke Charles is remembered. Flag in the hand, he plunged into the middle of the battle on his white horse and led his soldiers' charge. He did not "lead from behind," but demonstrated battle-changing bravery from the front, stopping the force of the French charge and turning the battle. Although the fighting continued to rage throughout the day, the archduke's heroic action had saved the day. By evening, Napoleon understood that he had lost: heavy Austrian barges were floating down the Danube, destroying the bridges of the French and endangering their safe retreat.

The French had suffered their first loss in ten years. Napoleon had lost his first land battle, ever. Moreover, his ablest general, Marshal Lannes, had died in the battle. Altogether, about forty thousand soldiers were killed on both sides, a horrible toll. However, because the French were able to repair some bridges and cross back over the Danube, they saved their army from being totally destroyed.

The Austrians were so surprised by their victory, and so exhausted by two days of battle, that they did not capitalize on their victory. Two months later, at the monumental Battle of Wagram, Charles had a re-match against Napoleon and lost. In fact, because he personally accepted a truce (after a second, smaller battle in Znaim five days later that further ravaged his troops), his brother the emperor relieved him of his command.

Charles retired from his military career and wasn't present for the final victories against Napoleon. Nowadays, people sometimes wonder what was so important about Aspern, particularly given the loss just two months later, but we have long forgotten what a thunderclap went through Europe after the Battle of Aspern. The battle proved that Napoleon could be beaten. This realization was an awakening. Until Aspern, Napoleon had seemed an unstoppable force of nature. Now everyone realized he was just a man who could be stopped. Aspern was the first victory that led ultimately to Leipzig and Waterloo. The many monuments, books, and ballads that commemorate this moment preserve some sense of what Charles' achievement at Aspern meant to his contemporaries.

The next time you are in Vienna, walk to the *Heldenplatz* and contemplate the famous equestrian statue of Charles in the middle of the battle.

Solferino

Fifty-five years later, on June 24, 1859, Emperor Franz Joseph decided to lead his troops himself, rather than delegate the task to a brilliant general, in the Battle of Solferino. He was no longer Emperor of the Holy Roman Empire, but only Emperor of Austria—so perhaps it seemed to him the appropriate thing to do.

The battle was the decisive moment in the war that the Austrians fought against the French and Piedmontese during the period of Italian unification called the *Risorgimento*. Solferino is a tiny village about ten miles south of Lake Garda in Northern Italy. The complicated battlefield actually comprised several villages; and the opposing sides warred for nearly thirteen continuous hours. In the end, the allies achieved a tactical victory against the Austrians. But there were tens of thousands of dead on both sides, and tens of thousands wounded. Both sides were shocked. Nearly forty thousand soldiers fell ill in the days after the battle. In fact, the majority of the war dead actually died after the battle. It was this appalling carnage after the battle that led to the Geneva Convention and indeed to the formation of the Red Cross.[27]

Most of all, it was clear that the tactical dispositions of the young and inexperienced emperor had played a crucial role in that

[27] The founder of the Red Cross, Henry Dunant, saw the aftermath of the battle. He was given a Nobel peace prize for his work.

defeat. He had never even tried to outflank the French left wing, and three of his Army corps were never really used in the battle.

In any case, Franz Joseph never personally commandeered a battle again but instead relied on his generals.

Emperor of Peace

He was called the "Emperor of Peace," but that did not mean that Blessed Karl avoided the battlefields. On the contrary. From the very first days of World War I, he toured the fronts as the "eyes and ears" of Emperor Franz Joseph. These were not secure, guarded visits. He exposed himself to real risk. In fact, Franz Joseph didn't like to see him go and once said, on a visit to see the future Empress Zita and the children: "I am a very old man and Otto is a child. What happens if something happens to Karl?"

Karl saw many theatres of war. He was on the Russian front, in the Przemyśl Fortress (now on the Polish-Ukraine border). But he also toured the other fronts, earning him the moniker *Karl der Plötzliche*, "Karl the Sudden," because he would suddenly appear. He impressed everybody with his knowledge and his modesty and shared the Spartan conditions of the soldiers despite his elevated social rank. Nevertheless, while he was touring, he was contemplating how he would use this future power to reform the army along the lines his uncle, the deceased heir Franz Ferdinand, had developed.

In March 1916, Karl saw real action in the "white hell" of the Alps in the war against the Italians. He was the commander of the Twentieth Edelweiss Corps of the Eleventh Army. The archduke was very popular among his men, and even rescued one of them during a flash flood; he secured the all-important Tyrolian passes; during a massive offensive in the Alps, he saw the Austrians smash through enemy lines until they couldn't move any further. (There are a few very impressive photographs from that time.)

As the Russians were advancing on July 1, 1916, he took command of the eponymous Army Group Archduke Karl in Galicia. With this very provisional force, he was able to stop the Russian advance.

In October 1916, he and his wife Zita inspected the troops at the Romanian front in Kolozsvár, Cluj. Romanian POWs were surprised when Zita greeted them in Romanian.

In mid-November, the couple rushed to Vienna: the emperor was gravely ill. Soon, he was dead. Karl was now the emperor himself. From that moment on, his experiences on the battlefield—experiences that few other rulers and statesmen had had—motivated him to work for peace, and only for peace, as fast as possible. In his accession speech he proclaimed: "I will do all within my power to banish the horrors and sacrifices of war at the earliest possible date and to win back for my peoples the sorely missed blessings of peace."

He was good to his word. Whenever opportunities for peace seemed possible, he tried to seize them, even at the cost of his reputation. Through his brother-in-law, Prince Sixtus of Bourbon, he reached out to the French discreetly and proposed peace negotiation, but, when this became public, he was heavily criticized. When Pope Benedict XV proposed a peace initiative, Karl immediately responded enthusiastically, but he was the only ruler to do so. When President Wilson proposed his fourteen-point demands, Karl was ready to accept all points. But again, Austria was tied to Germany—and the Germans wouldn't hear of peace. Had any of these peace initiatives been pursued, millions of lives might have been saved.

Do I want you, dear readers, to become soldiers and go into battle—or want our politicians all to put on a uniform? Of course not. I have enormous respect for soldiers, and I would encourage anyone to defend their country. But just as Karl was as tireless a worker for peace as he was a courageous soldier, I believe we all must be courageous and brave in all our battles, in whatever form life (or God) presents them.

RULE 7

DIE WELL

(and Have a Memorable Funeral)

I HAVE WITNESSED the "knocking ritual" — sometimes called the "Habsburg ritual" — twice in my life. The first time was in 1989, when Empress Zita died; the second time was in 2011, when Otto von Habsburg was laid to rest. Nobody who has witnessed this impressive ceremony is untouched by it.[28]

The coffin carrying a Habsburg's mortal remains arrives in the *Neuer Markt* square near the Habsburg palace in Vienna. It stops in front of the entrance to the Capuchin crypt (*Kapuzinergruft*) where Habsburgs have been buried for more than four hundred years. A huge crowd watches in silence as the master of ceremonies knocks three times on the door. The voice of a Capuchin friar answers from within:

"Who desires entry?"

The master of ceremonies proceeds to list all the titles of the deceased, for example: "Otto of Austria, once Crown Prince of Austria-Hungary; Royal Prince of Hungary and Bohemia; of

[28] You can see it yourself on YouTube. It is worth watching. It bears a certain similarity to the scene that Jesus describes in Luke 13:25.

Dalmatia, Croatia, Slavonia, Galicia, Lodomeria and Illyria." The list goes on for almost a full minute.

Then the voice from within answers slowly, "We do not know him."

The master of ceremonies knocks again three times, and once again he is asked, "Who desires entry?" This time the master of ceremonies lists all the deeds of the deceased Habsburg. The voice from within again replies, "We do not know him."

The master of ceremonies knocks three more times and finally to the question "Who desires entry?" he now answers: "Otto, a mortal and sinful man."

The friar finally responds, "Then let him come in." The door to the crypt slowly swings open.

We can't say with confidence when this old ritual was developed. My guess is that it happened in the seventeenth century just after the devout Emperor Leopold I (although the first question about the titles was originally read at street level while the rest of the conversation took place downstairs in front of the actual entrance of the crypt). But whenever it began, and whatever small changes it has undergone over the centuries, the ritual encapsulates the attitude the Habsburg family has always maintained towards death. It is very provocative and is designed to make us all reflect on our lives and to think about our own deaths.

In this very uncertain life, there is but one certainty: We will all die.

Every single one of us.

However, in today's world death seems at times to be almost forgotten, hidden away in hospitals and behind euphemistic words. For most of Habsburg history, however, dying and living were both very public affairs. In fact, death was one of the most important moments of life, one for which you prepared from childhood. As Catholics, the Habsburgs understood that, no matter how you had behaved over the course of your life, the way you died could be crucial to your salvation, and indeed could even determine how you were going to spend eternity. While some may have experienced death-bed conversions, this could by no means be the expectation. In fact, you were unlikely to spend your final hours in prayer and with the sacraments if you hadn't been practicing your faith during your lifetime.

We live in an age where almost everyone seems certain that they will go to Heaven. (As somebody once said, "nowadays the only thing you need to do to get to Heaven is to die.") Most people seem blissfully unaware that there is a possibility that they may end up in Hell for all eternity. In fact, I am frequently surprised at how casually priests at funerals provide assurances that the dearly departed is "with God." Priests rarely speak of Purgatory and almost never mention Hell. Presumably these pastors do not wish to burden family and friends with unpleasant possibilities. But perhaps they should remind people of the concrete things they can do for their departed loved ones, such as pray for their souls?

My Habsburg ancestors knew that in death they had to give a public example to their subjects of how a Catholic should die. More importantly, they knew that the moment of death was the last opportunity they would have to make things right with God. But they also knew that prayer could help them make the transition from Purgatory—where most believed they would go—to Heaven. They made sure that many, many people in monasteries, churches, and chapels would say Masses and prayers for the repose of their souls.

Let's exhume the lives of a few Habsburg souls and look closely at their deaths, to see their motivations and pay them our respects.

Maximilian

As we've seen, Emperor Maximilian was a larger-than-life figure—a knight, a writer, a lover, a hunter. At one point towards the end of his life, he even considered trying to become pope. (He told one of his children in a letter that he would "not lie with a naked woman anymore.") While nothing came of his grandiose plan, death did finally come. But Maximilian had prepared a number of testamentary post-mortem instructions to express his Christian faith. They may seem a bit outlandish to our sensibilities, but they were intended to reflect piety and to benefit his subjects.

First, he ordered that his corpse should be shorn of hair, flagellated, and have its teeth broken out. He ordered that his body should lie in that state publicly before burial, and he directed that portraits be painted of his remains in this condition.[29] He wanted to let the world know that even an emperor is but a poor sinner, in a manner reminiscent of the Knocking Ritual.

But there were other aspects of his faith he also wanted to express. He ordered that his favorite suit of armor be placed in a side chapel of the Cathedral in his beloved town of Innsbruck, kneeling, with its hands folded in prayer, in front of the Blessed Sacrament, forever. And it is indeed there to this day. The emperor's armor continues to provide an incredible example of Eucharistic piety—and no small dash of splendor.

Finally, he ordered his body to be buried under the steps of the high altar in the church of Wiener Neustadt (where he had spent his youth) so that when the priest said Holy Mass, he would lift the Body of Christ directly above Maximilian's chest and pray for his soul.

---

[29] There are several copies extant. One of them is in the Eggenberg Castle near Graz, Austria, which you can visit, or lookup online.

A lifetime of imperial pageantry had clearly taught Maximilian how to do things right. A number of his descendants learned his lessons well.

For example, two of Maximilian's grandchildren, Charles V and his successor Ferdinand I, both prepared intensively for their deaths and died as good Catholics. Charles spent his last years in a monastery, and his recorded last words were *ay, Jesus* ("oh, Jesus"). Ferdinand died "as a saint," wrote one contemporary observer. Ferdinand's daughter, Magdalena, became a venerable herself and had a very touching death as abbess of the Monastery of Hall in Tyrol, exhorting her nuns and dying amid the prayers of her community.

At the same time, not all of Maximilian's progeny behaved with such Catholic devotion. Emperor Maximilian II declined the sacraments for the dying (Confession and Extreme Unction, nowadays called Anointing of the Sick) on his deathbed. Although family members begged him to call a priest, he simply said "my priest is in Heaven." A similar situation occurred with his son and successor, Emperor Rudolf II. At three in the morning on January 20, 1613, it was clear that the emperor was dying. A priest was called, but according to several observers Rudolf also declined the sacraments like his father. He finally died at seven in the morning.

In the Spanish line, a most painful death was experienced by King Philip II. By the time his life ended in 1598, he had already been in pain for years. But at the very end, cancer ravaged his body, and for weeks he was in so much pain that he could barely be moved. However, he prayed to God to grant him a few days without pain before his death so he could do a full examination of conscience and confess himself in a complete way. His prayers were answered. He made his Confession—and then the pain resumed until the end.

It was under devout Emperor Ferdinand II that the tradition began of putting the bodies of the Habsburgs into the Capucine Crypt, their entrails under St. Stephen's Cathedral, and their hearts under the *Augustinerkirche*. What seems grotesque to our modern sensibilities made perfect sense to the Habsburg rulers. Not only did putting their "hearts in the *Augustinerkirche*" symbolize their love for Mary, but distributing one's body into three places ensured that more people would be praying for the family and the repose of one's soul.

It will not surprise us that when deeply pious Leopold I died in 1705, it was in a Catholic way. Masses were read in his room all the time (and all through the empire), he loudly and clearly repeated the prayers of the dying—and he confessed shortly before he died. In fact, while praying and before Confession the priest asked him:

> *"Intelligitne Vestra Majestas quae dico?"*
> *"Ita, mi pater."*
> *("Does Your Majesty understand what I say?"*
> *"Yes, my Father.")*

We remember from the "Be Catholic" chapters that his was the pinnacle of Habsburg Baroque piety. Having been taught early on to prepare for death, Leopold received it relaxed and in devotion.

One of Empress Maria Theresia's daughters, Josefa, contracted smallpox in 1767 when she was twelve years old. Smallpox was known to bring death or permanent disfigurement, so she immediately asked for the priest and delivered a life Confession. She did die soon afterwards, but she was prepared. I am impressed at how even Habsburg children had their priorities right.

Empress Maria Theresia herself died in 1780, strengthened by the sacraments and surrounded by her praying family.

When her son Joseph II died on the morning of February 20, the Enlightenment man who had done so much damage to the Church had had his confessor with him the entire last day of his life. After a fainting episode on the morning of February 19, he called for him. On the morning of February 20, he called him again. The priest read to him from a pious book, and then Joseph died five minutes later.

Marie Antoinette, the daughter of Maria Theresia and the ill-fated wife of the last king of France, Louis XVI, has been unfairly treated by history. Though historians have long pointed out that she never said "Let them eat cake," she is nevertheless perceived as having been vain and superficial. In fact, Marie Antoinette, like her husband, was very devout. While her faith may have been somewhat formalistic at times (perhaps due to the rather rigorous maternal instructions in letters), in the last months and days of her life her Catholic faith shone brilliantly.

Revolutionary leaders had refused to let her see a Catholic priest for Confession before her execution. She could only pray in front of her little crucifix. The revolutionaries may not have intended to be cruel. Perhaps they simply couldn't allow a priest who hadn't taken the oath on the Revolution anywhere near the queen. But for her, this was a catastrophe. How could she go to God if she had not been properly reconciled with him?

We have the testimony of the executioner of Paris, Charles-Henri Sanson, so we know exactly what he said happened on the day of her death. It is very moving. In that famous moment during which the painter David hastily sketched the last portrait of the French queen, Sanson the executioner sat with her on the cart, on its way to the guillotine, through the jeering crowds. He testifies that Marie Antoinette was nervous and troubled as the cart moved through the winding streets. She kept turning her head back and forth and seemed to be looking for something along the way. Finally, after they had passed a certain house, she was suddenly totally in peace. And in that peace, she went to her death — after asking her executioner to pardon her for having stepped on his foot accidentally while climbing the scaffold. Sanson later learned, from faithful Catholics who had remained in France during the revolution, the reason for her astonishing change of behavior. She had been told that at a window of one of the houses on the way to the guillotine there would be a Catholic bishop in disguise who would, from that window, impart an absolution *in extremis* to her. The moment she had seen him, she knew that all would be well, and she was prepared to die.

Emperor Franz Joseph, on November 21, 1916, saw to it that he died in a very Catholic way. Having suffered from a high fever for some time, he went to Holy Mass and Confession in the morning. Towards lunchtime, his devout daughter Marie Valerie visited him. He told her — with little pauses caused by the exertion — that he had not only confessed, but also gone to Mass and taken Communion "as this is important." He knew it was particularly important to her and wanted to assure her that he had done these things. At eight in the evening, he received Extreme Unction. Marie Valerie was at his side holding a crucifix for him to kiss over and over. Also present were Bl. Emperor Karl and his wife, Zita. In his feverish state, Franz Joseph ordered his servant Ketterl to wake him early the next morning for work. The emperor died that night.

However, in the eight hundred years of our family, the maxim "die well" may have been achieved best by Bl. Emperor Karl, the loving father and mild-spoken last Emperor of Austria. Shortly after he arrived in Madeira in exile in 1922, he contracted pneumonia. Perhaps it was caused by the foggy, humid climate that hung over the hill where his house stood. In any case, within a few weeks, his pneumonia got worse, and he suffered and died.

But there are several ways in which Blessed Karl's death was quite singular. When he was already in Madeira, but before he caught the illness, he seems to have offered his life, and his suffering, to God for his people. The pain he endured from various treatments — which were intended to help but which only made matters worse — is hard to imagine (though it is poignantly described in the little booklet, *Death of an Emperor* (which I frequently recommend). But through all his terrible suffering, he remained calm, humble, and accepting. His secret? He was constantly in prayer. "If one didn't have prayer or the devotion to the Sacred Heart, all of this would not be tolerable," he once muttered. He had Mass said in his room or in the adjacent room so he could see the Blessed Sacrament while he was suffering.

During a feverish attack he said, "I must suffer so much so my people can be together." I sometimes wonder how many political leaders nowadays would see their suffering in this light. When it came to the end, Karl called in his son Otto so he would see "how an Emperor dies." He died, whispering the prayers of the dying, in the arms of his wife, with the final word "Jesus" on his lips.

Karl's manner of death would never have occurred in a soul that had not been shaped by a life of daily Holy Mass, frequent rosary prayer, devotion to the Sacred Heart, and regular Confession. But the manner in which Karl accepted suffering and death helped make him a blessed of the Church. In a family of emperors, he received an even higher honor — and he is the only person in our family who has. He showed us all that "Die Well" means live well, too. To understand almost everything the

Habsburgs did and do, you must realize that they—that we—have always thought about life, duties, politics, and faith with an eye towards the end.

Perhaps that's why a Roman poet once said: *Quidquid agis, prudenter agas, et respice finem* ("Whatever you do, do it wisely and keep the end in sight"). We should all take a moment and ask ourselves whether our end figures as prominently in our thoughts as it, inevitably, will.

And then pray to God for His help.

HABSBURGS TODAY

THE DEATH OF Bl. Karl in April 1922 was not the end of the Habsburgs. Hardly. In fact, the adventures of the widowed young Empress Zita and her eight children (Otto, Adelheid, Robert, Felix, Carl-Ludwig, Rudolph, Charlotte, and Elisabeth) in the decades after the death of the emperor would make an exciting book or Netflix series.

Zita

In the aftermath of WWI, the Allies did not wish to look after the Habsburgs, so the King of Spain took the pregnant widow and her seven children to Spain where her daughter Elisabeth was born. Eventually, Zita moved the family to Brussels to be closer to her Luxembourg cousins. But in both countries, they led a very strict life with daily Holy Mass, much studying, and many visits from devoted friends.

Zita kept a watchful eye on Austria. For a while at least, restoration of the monarchy seemed a distinct possibility, though as the decades passed, it became more and more unlikely. In 1930, when Otto had his eighteenth birthday, he became the head of the Habsburg family. A decade later, when Germany invaded Belgium, Zita's family fled, first to France, then to Spain, then to Portugal, and finally to North America.

They lived at first in Catholic Quebec, but then moved to Tuxedo Park, New York, and lived there throughout the forties. Some of Zita's sons returned to Europe to fight Hitler as soldiers and in the resistance—a whole chapter (or Netflix season) in the Habsburg Adventure series could be made of their efforts. After the war, the Empress went back to Europe. When her children had all married, she moved into an old-age home for religious, where she lived from 1962 until her death in 1989.

It was there that I had the privilege of visiting her as a child. It was very memorable and most impressive. She received our family in a little salon, dressed all in black. She spoke a melodious, clear, old-fashioned Austrian. (Her voice is preserved in YouTube videos.) Her body looked fragile. But you could sense the rod of moral steel that kept her straight, and she had a gentle and warm-hearted way about her. What impressed me most was her social grace and the way she made sure everybody in the room was involved in the conversation, even the youngest. It was the way she had been doing things since she herself was a young empress, traveling through the empire. You never forgot you were in the presence of a queen and empress.

She told us many little details about the coronation in Budapest that I will never forget—for instance, that it was very difficult for the emperor to keep the crown on his head as the soft protective inner ring had not been put in, so the crown slipped back and forth on his head. She also offered us chocolates that tasted horrible, like soap. We discovered later that she often received chocolate boxes as gifts, never ate them, and eventually offered the old boxes of chocolates to her guests—after they had spent months lying on top of a cupboard.

Before Zita died, at the ripe old age of ninety-six years, she was allowed to return to Austria several times. Her funeral in 1989 was as close as you could get to a state funeral from the Austro-Hungarian monarchy—and included the famous "knocking ritual" at the door of the Capucine Crypt.

Otto

I have quoted Dr. Otto von Habsburg quite a few times, sometimes without naming him, and a number of the ideas in this book are inspired by his speeches. The eldest son of Blessed Karl, Otto's life spanned the entire twentieth century, and he played a key role in it. He never moped around lamenting the empire he didn't have. Rather, he applied many of the historic Habsburg principles in the twentieth century circumstances in which he found himself, as he threw himself head-first into modern European politics. In fact, he was so energetic and involved in so many aspects of modern Europe he was sometimes called "The Uncrowned Emperor."

In the first decades of Otto's life, the titanic struggle with Adolf Hitler was the dominant theme.[30] Hitler hated many of the things that the young Habsburg heir stood for, from his Christian convictions to his belief that different nationalities and races could live happily together under one political roof. Otto had, of course, read Hitler's book *Mein Kampf.* (Many people had the book but very few actually bothered to read it.) Otto knew that Hitler would go after Austria after he had secured Germany. And fighting for the rights and liberty of Austria, and its central European neighbors, became Otto's mission.

---

[30] Charles Coulombe's excellent book *Blessed Charles of Austria: A Holy Emperor and His Legacy* (2020) provides a far more detailed narrative of the brief summary that follows.

Just before the *Anschluss*, Austrian Chancellor Kurt von Schuschnigg had met secretly with Otto in Switzerland. There had been some talk of a restoration of the Habsburgs, but Otto was certain this would never happen. Hitler would simply not allow it. In fact, when Hitler invaded Austria, the operation was named *Unternehmen Otto* ("Operation Otto"), Hitler's way of preempting the restoration discussions.

From the moment of the *Anschluss*, Otto moved tirelessly through Europe lobbying for Austrian independence. His efforts finally brought him to the White House, where he met President Roosevelt in 1940. That meeting led, among other things, to the founding in 1942 of a so-called "Free Austrian Battalion" to fight the Nazis. Two of Otto's brothers, Karl-Ludwig and Felix, immediately joined the battalion. At the same time, Otto himself was coordinating efforts with many resistance movements all over Europe and in Austria. After Pearl Harbor, his friendship with Roosevelt helped him secure the status of "friendly alien" for many Austrian POW's, which unfroze their bank accounts. He also managed to convince the Allies not to carry out a few bombing raids that would have hit Austria.

In the meantime, his brothers Rudolf, Felix, and Carl-Ludwig made it (with false papers from the French resistance) into Austria to join the resistance there. Their actions in 1944 and 1945 remain a book to be written. I quote Coulombe:

"The Resistance in the Tyrol with whom they fought were in large part monarchists, fighting in both North and South Tyrol, which word from London led them to believe would be returned to Austria after the war. In the beginning, they primarily performed acts of sabotage; they stepped up the attacks after June of 1944 and the Normandy invasion. But in May of 1945, when German tactics changed to blowing up bridges and other strategic facilities, the archdukes and their comrades-in-arms fought to save them."[31]

Although Otto was very active during WWII, it was his fight for a unified Europe after the war—and especially his commitment to including the countries of Central Europe in the Union—that are Otto's true legacy. His most famous phrase was *Paneuropa ist ganz Europa* ("Pan Europe is all of Europe"). At the time, large parts of Europe were behind the Iron Curtain, and for many people it was madness to think this would ever change. But then suddenly it did, when the curtain collapsed in 1989. Today, nobody is surprised that Latvia and Hungary are in the EU, but Otto saw the possibility long before others.

From the birth of the Paneuropa Union, in 1952, Otto fought for a united Europe—though one that preserved (as you may appreciate if you've read this book attentively) political subsidiarity. In 1973, Otto became the head of the International Paneuropa Movement, and in 1979 he was elected into the European Parliament for the first time. There he engaged directly in European politics, never forgetting his dear countries of *Mitteleuropa*. For example, he insisted that symbolic seats in the Parliament be kept empty for the future for countries still trapped behind the Iron Curtain.[32]

---

[31] Coulombe, Charles. *Blessed Charles of Austria*, 316.

[32] Despite Otto's commitment to modern Europe, his colleagues never forgot who he was. In fact, there is a funny story told about him. One day during a football match, everybody from Austria was very excited. Otto asked absent-mindedly, "Who's playing?"

"Austria-Hungary."

"Against whom?" came his answer.

Alas, the story is just a bit of fun. (I personally checked with Otto and he said he never said it; the story has also been told about Emperor Franz Joseph.) But joking aside, Otto's colleagues had enormous respect for him and all that he accomplished.

On August 19, 1989, Otto organized the famous Paneuropa-Picknick at the Austro-Hungarian border, near Sopron. His daughter Walburga (as well as the author of this book) was present when several hundred East-German refugees escaped through the opened Iron Curtain. The Austrian and Hungarian government had agreed to open the border fence at a place near Sopron to allow the Hungarian "Paneuropeans" to cross over and join the picnic on the other side of the fence. This was the official part. However, the Paneuropa Union had been advertising this picnic with flyers near the German Embassy in Hungary and the churches of the Order of Malta in Budapest where hundreds of East-German refugees had been camping for weeks. A large group of these refugees had travelled to the border and, when the fence was opened, they rushed to the west. Afterwards, Walburga and I spoke to the guard at that small border crossing. He told us: "I saw this huge crowd and had two possibilities: Shoot or turn the other direction. I did the latter."

It was the first tear in the border, and, as Otto himself once famously said, "The Iron Curtain is like a lady's stocking: one seam tears open and it will split." Indeed, it was only a few months later that the Berlin Wall fell, which in turn led to the collapse of the communist block in Eastern Europe.

Lotsa Habsburgs ...

When Otto died at ninety-eight years old in 2011, Vienna saw once again the traditional burial that culminated in the entrance to the *Kapuzinergruft*. But another epoch had ended. Still, the family goes on. Otto's son Karl is now head of our family, and also head of the Order of the Golden Fleece. Someday, his eldest son Ferdinand will succeed him. As I've said before, we are a traditional bunch.

Of course, Zita and her children were not the only members of the family to create a Habsburg legacy. Many other Habsburgs from the different lines are still around. In fact, on nearly all continents, you will find hundreds of them. We all live now in the twenty-first century and even have a WhatsApp group where many of us meet regularly. We also have family gatherings that bring together hundreds of family members, like the 2022 centenary of the death of Bl. Karl, in Madeira. You will find Habsburgs in all walks of life and all manner of work. We are nurses and movie makers; we work in museums and in banks; we are organic farmers and Red Cross workers and geographers, doctors, mothers, UN envoys, priests, and writers.

We have one very talented race car driver: our future head of family, Ferdinand.

I myself, after having done many other jobs, have become a diplomat (like several of my cousins). I work for one of those central European countries that, for many, remains a beacon of hope in today's chaotic world—and if you have read the seven points of the "Habsburg Way" carefully, you will see that quite a few of the rules are indeed manifested in the affairs of Hungarian politics. Hungary, like Poland, is blessed to have political leaders who live their faith visibly. Indeed, Christian faith has a very active presence in our public square. Hungary embraces policies that encourage families to have more children. Hungary strongly believes in subsidiarity with respect to international bodies. And most importantly, Hungary takes law and justice very seriously. If there is any country in Europe that "knows who they are," it is Hungary. It is not for nothing that it has two Habsburg Ambassadors in its services.

In fact, while so many other European countries seem to be struggling with their identities, it is curious that Hungary (and Poland) is sometimes accused of failing to exhibit European values. But Prime Minister Viktor Orbán's response to this change was absolutely correct when he remarked in his speech in Rome during his visit to the Pope in 2022: "They say we don't share

European values. If the founders of the European Union like Adenauer, Schumann, de Gasperi, would return today, where would they find the European values: in Brussels or in central Europe?"

We Habsburgs still stand for traditional family values and live by them. Many of us are married. Families with numerous children are the rule rather than the exception. The old family joke still holds that "Habsburg is a plural word and never exists in the singular." I myself just recently had the joy of organizing our first family wedding for one of my daughters. (No, her husband isn't a cousin, and, I promise, it wasn't arranged. Or was it?)

Another little detail about our family might make you smile: While our head of the family won't allow or forbid marriages anymore, it is a tradition to make the gesture of asking his consent when we get engaged. I most certainly did. I hope the younger generation will too.

Are we waiting for the monarchy to return? No. (Or are we?) But perhaps service is what we have in our genes, what we can do best, given the right circumstances. To everything there is a season, and at least in Austria and Central Europe, now is not the time for imperial restoration. But as you've seen through this book, forms may change but our values are still lived in today's society, and they will surely apply to lives lived one hundred years from now as well.

As we all know, history may not repeat itself, but it does rhyme. So we remain eager to discover what the future holds. Our head of family, Charles, once quoted a pop song by the band Wir sind Helden: "*Wir sind gekommen um zu bleiben*" ("We have come in order to stay around"). When the Habsburg family paid a visit to Pope Francis in 2016, I took a picture of our three-hundred-person clan filling the entire *Via della Conciliazione* after that audience. A high Vatican official saw the picture—filled with lots of kids—and said to me: "It looks like your family is going to be around for a looooong time."

... but what about you?

This brings us to the end of *The Habsburg Way*. I hope you have gotten to know my family much better over the pages of this volume. The next time you stroll through Vienna, or see a painting in a museum of somebody with a large chin, or notice a golden sheep dangling around his neck, you will smile knowingly and explain to your friends some of our story. You will also, I hope, remember some of the ideas and virtues that have shaped our history.

But even more, I hope that you will try to implement some of the Habsburg Way into your life. Everyone can at least aspire to find a spouse who is not just exceedingly good looking (like mine!) but someone who shares your values and your vision — and your ideas about children, your family, and your future. My experience is that this is considerably easier if you get to know the other person before you become intimate with them. Wait for intimacy until you are married! (Funnily enough, Catholic morals on sexuality for several millennia seem to have understood that pretty well.)

Work hard on your faith. Many of my ancestors did. It will improve your life and happiness, as it did theirs. Faith will also help you and your spouse to confront all the vicissitudes of life that will inevitably come your way. (And don't forget the old joke: You get married to confront, together, the problems that you wouldn't have had if you didn't get married.) Faith will also give you a compass in everyday life to make good decisions and to respond to the complex issues that constantly arise in any society. And it will help as you approach the one certitude in life: death. Remember to prepare for eternity during your life and to pray for final perseverance. With God's grace, at the end you will be able to withstand the final test.

Stand for law and justice. In the long run, your sense of purpose will make you really happy, even if in the short run it puts challenges in your way. For instance, do not cheat: not on your taxes, not at cards. Don't lie, even if that leads to very difficult situations. Look out for your wife and children, and your work colleagues, even if that sometimes means putting their welfare above your own.

Stand for your subjects. Even if you don't literally have "subjects" (most people don't these days), adjust the maxim to your own life. For those of us in the political sphere or the military, think of your constituents, or those under your command. For those who are teachers, on any level, stand for your students. Owners and managers of commercial organizations, stand for your employees. If God has placed you in any position of authority, no matter how great or small, use your gifts for the good of those you govern. Remember, "dealing well with them" is not only your duty, it can affect your salvation.

Believe in subsidiarity. It will give you a map to judge politics, to see whether there is a real respect for the "lower" and "more local" level.

Finally, know who you are. As I said before, you must know who you are if you are not going to be blown over when the whirlwind comes. The temptation to go with the flow, to be accepted—even if it causes you unease—is very great in us, weak humans that we are. Adhering to tried, tested, and traditional values in your life will give you security and a vision. It will also allow you to stand up for others, to take a microphone in front of an angry crowd—and still to stand up for your beliefs.

But what about society?

What about our political leaders and our society? Wouldn't they also profit from applying the Habsburg Way to it? Yes indeed.

A government that encourages marriage and childbearing helps to build a stable society. A government that promotes Christian religious values, even in public, encourages its citizens to live an ethical life and not simply to consume and exist in an egotistical way. Political leaders who remember that even they are mortal and will one day have to defend their deeds before God will be more apt to act in a good way.

Political leaders that stand for law, justice, and their citizens will foster confidence in the state and encourage similar behaviors in "regular" people. We have gotten so accustomed to corruption in political circles that we have a hard time imagining a system where honest men and women act in the interest of the people. Wouldn't it be wonderful if we had politicians and political leaders who were our role models again—rather than simply Hollywood stars with their endless kaleidoscope of woke fads?

If international institutions respected subsidiarity, many of them would work much better—in particular, the European Union would. But the United States, which was built on the promise of subsidiarity, has also become highly centralized as well. This is rightly making Americans uneasy. Many people sense that distant global forces are interfering with their local institutions, laws, and habits. Giving the lower, more local levels their proper sphere of responsibility would help raise the confidence of the population in their elected leaders.

The Habsburg family has shown how to implement these values over the course of many centuries and in many very different situations. So ask for these values from your politicians. Demand them. And the next time a politician does something outlandish, ask yourself: What would a Habsburg do now?

ACKNOWLEDGMENTS

As I SAID at the start, this is not an academic history book full of obscure footnotes. This is a collection of family stories and things I have heard, read, and seen over many years. However, if you would like to learn more, I can suggest a few volumes. I ask pardon in advance if, among the short list of the books here, I owe a debt to any resource that I have forgotten to mention.

The best, most comprehensive book to read about the family history is without doubt: Martyn Rady's, *The Habsburgs: The Rise and Fall of a World Power*, 2020. I have used stories and quoted from Rady's book a lot. I also highly recommend his shorter and snappier introduction (which I have also referenced): *The Habsburg Empire: A Very Short Introduction*, Oxford University Press, 2017.

Dorothy Gies McGuigan's *The Hapsburgs*, Doubleday, 1966, is an excellent companion to Rady's book. Where Rady is concerned primarily with the broader history of the Empire, Gies McGuigan highlights personal stories, Habsburg family life, and the Faith. You really get to know individual family members, and she really seems to love them herself. It's a very enjoyable read.

Every Habsburg enthusiast's library should include Charles Coulombe's *Blessed Charles of Austria: A Holy Emperor and His*

Legacy, TAN Books, 2020. This book is not only an excellent and highly readable biography of the last Habsburg Emperor, it is also a good introduction to the Habsburg idea of Empire—and a good primer on Habsburg devotion and piety.

Otto von Habsburg's *Idee Europa* and *Die Reichsidee* are collections of speeches and articles that I consulted to understand some of the larger political themes. However, those are in German.

There are many other books, biographies, and other works about the Habsburgs that I have perused over many years. There are also a few prominent old and new books about the Habsburgs that I have not read but that I would like to mention because they are so well-regarded by others: *The Habsburg Empire, A New History*, by Pieter M. Judson, Belknap Press, 2018; *The Grand Strategy of the Habsburg Empire* by A. Wess Mitchell, Princeton University Press, 2019; and any of the books written by Gordon Brook-Shepherd about the Habsburgs. A fascinating read on the relations between the United States and the Habsburgs is Jonathan Singerton's recent *The American Revolution and the Habsburg Monarchy*, University of Virginia Press, 2022.

Finally, the idea for this book was born in Boston, in April 2022, thanks to an invitation by Christopher Laconi to give a talk about Habsburg values to the Somerset Club. The parameters he gave me were the basis of the talk and eventually the basis of this tome. Thank you, Christopher. Also, without the enthusiasm and encouragement of George Gunning and Vincenzo La Ruffa, I would never have believed in this project enough to complete it. To Bertalan: The Emperor protects! Finally, my sincere thanks to Sophia Press for publishing my love letter to my family.

About the Author

Eduard Habsburg is Hungary's ambassador to the Holy See and the Sovereign Order of Malta. His family reigned in Austria, Hungary, Germany, Spain (and quite a few other places). Also known as Archduke Eduard of Austria, he is a diplomat and social media personality. Eduard and his wife, Baroness Maria Theresia von Gudenus, have six children. Eduard is the author of several books, including the children's book *Dubbie: The Double-Headed Eagle*; volumes on Thomas Aquinas, James Bond, and Harry Potter; novels; and screenplays.

THE
NEUMANN ✠ FORUM

The Mission
The Neumann Forum unites and engages faithful
Catholics who are dedicated to preserving and
protecting the Catholic Faith.

Sophia Institute

SOPHIA INSTITUTE IS a nonprofit institution that seeks to nurture the spiritual, moral, and cultural life of souls and to spread the gospel of Christ in conformity with the authentic teachings of the Roman Catholic Church.

Sophia Institute Press fulfills this mission by offering translations, reprints, and new publications that afford readers a rich source of the enduring wisdom of mankind.

Sophia Institute also operates the popular online resource CatholicExchange.com. *Catholic Exchange* provides world news from a Catholic perspective as well as daily devotionals and articles that will help readers to grow in holiness and live a life consistent with the teachings of the Church.

In 2013, Sophia Institute launched Sophia Institute for Teachers to renew and rebuild Catholic culture through service to Catholic education. With the goal of nurturing the spiritual, moral, and cultural life of souls, and an abiding respect for the role and work of teachers, we strive to provide materials and programs that are at once enlightening to the mind and ennobling to the heart; faithful and complete, as well as useful and practical.

Sophia Institute gratefully recognizes the Solidarity Association for preserving and encouraging the growth of our apostolate over the course of many years. Without their generous and timely support, this book would not be in your hands.

www.SophiaInstitute.com
www.CatholicExchange.com
www.SophiaInstituteforTeachers.org

Sophia Institute Press is a registered trademark of Sophia Institute.
Sophia Institute is a tax-exempt institution as defined by the
Internal Revenue Code, Section 501(c)(3). Tax ID 22-2548708.